BAPTISTWAYPRESS®

Adult Bible Study Guide

The Book of Acts

Toward Being a
Missional Church

Dennis Foust
William Tinsley
Brian Harbour

BAPTISTWAYPRESS®

Dallas, Texas

BAPTISTWAY PRESS® Management Team
Executive Director, Baptist General Convention of Texas: Charles Wade
Director, Missions, Evangelism, and Ministry Team: Wayne Shuffield
Ministry Team Leader: Phil Miller
Publisher, BAPTISTWAY PRESS®: Ross West

Cover and Interior Design and Production: Desktop Miracles, Inc.
Printing: Data Reproductions Corporation
Cover Photo: The Acropolis in Athens, www.bibleplaces.com

First edition: March 2007
ISBN-10: 1–931060–87–8
ISBN-13: 978-1-931060-87-5

How to Make the Best Use of This Issue

Whether you're the teacher or a student—

1. Start early in the week before your class meets.
2. Overview the study. Review the table of contents and read the study introduction. Try to see how each lesson relates to the overall study.
3. Use your Bible to read and consider prayerfully the Scripture passages for the lesson. (You'll see that each writer has chosen a favorite translation for the lessons in this issue. You're free to use the Bible translation you prefer and compare it with the translation chosen for that unit, of course.)
4. After reading all the Scripture passages in your Bible, then read the writer's comments. The comments are intended to be an aid to your study of the Bible.
5. Read the small articles—"sidebars"—in each lesson. They are intended to provide additional, enrichment information and inspiration and to encourage thought and application.
6. Try to answer for yourself the questions included in each lesson. They're intended to encourage further thought and application, and they can also be used in the class session itself.

If you're the teacher—

A. Do all of the things just mentioned, of course. In the first session of the study, briefly overview the study by identifying with your class the date on which each lesson will be studied. Lead your class to write the date in the table of contents on page 7 and on the first page of each lesson. You might also find it helpful to make and post a chart that indicates the date on which each lesson will be studied. If all of your class has e-mail, send them an e-mail with the dates the lessons will be studied. (At least one church that uses BAPTISTWAY® materials for its classes places a sticker on the table of contents to identify the dates.) *Note*: An Easter lesson is included. If your class uses the Easter lesson, you may need to decide how to study the other lessons, such as by combining two lessons or studying the missed lesson at a special class meeting.

B. Get a copy of the *Teaching Guide*, a companion piece to this *Study Guide*. The *Teaching Guide* contains additional Bible comments plus two teaching plans. The teaching plans in the *Teaching Guide* are intended to provide practical, easy-to-use teaching suggestions that will work in your class.

C. After you've studied the Bible passage, the lesson comments, and other material, use the teaching suggestions in the *Teaching Guide* to help you develop your plan for leading your class in studying each lesson.

D. You may want to get the additional adult Bible study comments— *Adult Online Bible Commentary*—by Dr. Jim Denison, pastor of Park Cities Baptist Church, Dallas, Texas, that are available at www.baptistwaypress.org and can be downloaded free. An additional teaching plan plus teaching resource items are also available at www.baptistwaypress.org.

E. You also may want to get the enrichment teaching help that is provided on the internet by the *Baptist Standard* at www.baptiststandard.com. (Other class participants may find this information helpful, too.) Call 214–630–4571 to begin your subscription to the printed edition of the *Baptist Standard*.

F. Enjoy leading your class in discovering the meaning of the Scripture passages and in applying these passages to their lives.

Writers of This Study Guide

Dennis Foust, pastor of Shades Crest Baptist Church, Birmingham, Alabama, wrote the Easter lesson and unit one, lessons 1–4. Other churches Dr. Foust has served as pastor or associate pastor include Second-Ponce de Leon, Atlanta, Georgia; First, Chattanooga, Tennessee; and Manor, San Antonio, Texas. He received his master's and doctoral degrees from The Southern Baptist Theological Seminary, Louisville, Kentucky.

William (Bill) Tinsley wrote unit two, lessons 5–8. He serves as the leader of WorldconneX, the missions network created by the Baptist General Convention of Texas (BGCT). Prior to this, he served as associate executive director of the BGCT; executive director of the Minnesota-Wisconsin Baptist Convention; director of missions in Denton Association, Texas; and pastor for sixteen years.

Brian Harbour, writer of unit three, lessons 9–13, is pastor of First Baptist Church, Richardson, Texas. Dr. Harbour served previously at Immanuel Baptist Church, Little Rock, Arkansas; First Baptist Church, Pensacola, Florida; Shiloh Terrace Baptist Church, Dallas, Texas; Colonial Heights Baptist Church, Jackson, Mississippi; and Woodland Hills Baptist Church, Atlanta, Georgia. He is a graduate of Baylor University (B.A.; Ph.D.).

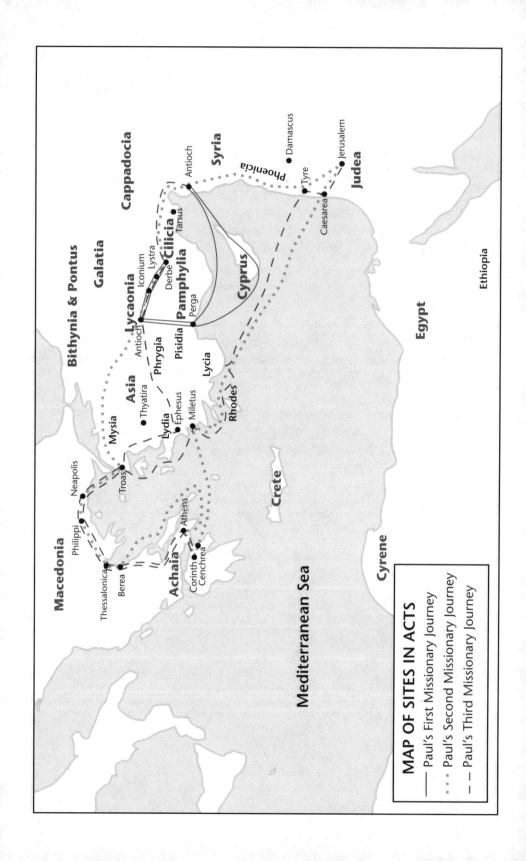

MAP OF SITES IN ACTS

—— Paul's First Missionary Journey

· · · · Paul's Second Missionary Journey

– – – Paul's Third Missionary Journey

The Book of Acts: Toward Being a Missional Church

Date of Study

UNIT ONE

Growing in Strength

UNIT TWO

Moving Outward

U N I T   T H R E E

On Mission to the World

THE BOOK OF ACTS:
Toward Being a Missional Church

One church leader, observing the situation in churches in general today, suggested, "For many people within North America the church is a place where individuals go passively to receive religious goods and services."[1] Do you think that's true? When we think of how casually people, even active Christians, talk about "going to church," we recognize that's how we tend to think of church—a place we go "to receive religious goods and services." Dietrich Bonhoeffer, the German Christian martyred for his faith during the closing days of World War II, captured a similar thought when he wrote, stating the attitude of a nominal Christian, " . . . My only duty as a Christian is to leave the world for an hour or so on a Sunday morning and go to church to be assured that my sins are all forgiven."[2]

While the expressions in the previous paragraph seem true, let us recognize that sometimes people simply use the words "going to church" as shorthand for the experiences of worship, fellowship, learning, and giving—including giving to missions—that may occur there. The church to which they go may even be involved—heavily involved—in missions, in sending out money or even people to "do mission work."

In recent years, though, many people who are concerned about and committed to the church have pointed out that even that approach to church does not capture what God intends the church to be about. Thus, the words *missional church* are being used to describe what God intends the church to be and do. What is meant by the words *missional church*? Is your church a *missional church*?

A Missional Church?

For the missional church, missions is not simply another program or activity. Rather, it is what the church is and does; it participates fully in God's mission. So in a missional church, missions is not what most members of the church rely on other people to do or what they give to so that other people can do missions. Rather, in a missional church, missions is what the members themselves do.

As one Baptist author has stated, "the missional church emphasizes *being* and *doing*." Instead of just sending and supporting others, "the missional church is *participative*." In fact, mission is not just one way the church ministers. Rather, "the missional church perceives mission as *the essence of its existence*."[3] In summary, the missional church is "a reproducing community of authentic disciples, being equipped as missionaries sent by God, to live and proclaim His Kingdom in the world."[4] Further, as another Baptist leader wrote, "Missional churches . . . see their purpose for existence as incarnating the life and ministry of Jesus Christ and thus extending the mission of God."[5]

The Missional Church in the New Testament

When people who are committed to the work of the church see such definitions of the *missional church*, they likely realize that the idea is not new, although the word may be. The idea surely dates to the New Testament. In fact, the missional church is the church we find in the New Testament. The missional church is the church we see in action in the Book of Acts and in the early centuries of the Christian era.

The missional church is the church that served its Lord before the idea of *Christendom* took hold, which occurred beginning about the fourth century A.D. The change occurred most noticeably when the Roman emperor Constantine, having become a Christian, granted freedom to Christianity and at the same time took a leading role in controlling the church. The church thus became socially respectable and participated in the power of the culture. As a result, in the culture of Christendom, everybody knows that the church is a place you go—or the place you're supposed to go— and missions is what you send someone else to do way over there or out there. Not so in the early days of the church in the Book of Acts, and not so in most of our world now.

The reality is that the church of Christendom no longer exists in most parts of what was known as the Christian world or at least it is fading fast or is spotty in its influence. Our culture is changing. Ideas are being questioned. The church finds itself having to justify its existence to the larger world. Too, the people of the world who need the good news of Christ are no longer far away but can be found at our own door. Indeed, the mission field begins at the church door.

Now we are more and more in the situation of the early Christians. To be faithful Christians and churches today, we will need to learn to operate in the same way our early Christian brothers and sisters did. We must recognize that missions begins here, and Christians—not just "missionaries," but all Christians—are the ones who must do it. We are the ones who are sent to do God's mission.

Studying the Missional Church in Acts

This study is, of course, on the Book of Acts. In studying this book, we will focus on what we can learn from our early Christian brothers and sisters about how to grow toward being a missional church. The study is

---

Additional Resources for Studying the Book of Acts[7]

F. F. Bruce. *The Book of the Acts.* The New International Commentary on the New Testament. Grand Rapids, Michigan: Eerdmans, 1988.

Richard N. Longenecker. "Acts." *The Expositor's Bible Commentary.* Grand Rapids, Michigan: Zondervan, 1981.

J. W. MacGorman. *Acts: The Gospel for All People.* Nashville, Tennessee: Convention Press, 1990.

Howard Marshall. *Acts.* Tyndale New Testament Commentaries. Grand Rapids, Michigan: Eerdmans, 1980.

John B. Polhill. *Acts.* The New American Commentary. Volume 26. Nashville, Tennessee: Broadman Press, 1992.

A. T. Robertson. *Word Pictures in the New Testament.* Volume III. Nashville, Tennessee: Broadman Press, 1930.

T.C. Smith. *Acts.* The Broadman Bible Commentary. Volume 10. Nashville, Tennessee: Broadman Press, 1970.

Frank Stagg. *The Book of Acts: The Early Struggle for an Unhindered Gospel.* Nashville, Tennessee: Broadman Press, 1955.

John R. W. Stott. *The Message of Acts.* The Bible Speaks Today. Downers Grove, Illinois: InterVarsity, 1994.

William H. Willimon. *Acts.* Interpretation: A Bible Commentary for Teaching and Preaching. Atlanta: John Knox Press, 1988.

---

organized along the lines suggested in Acts 1:8—"You will receive power when the Holy Spirit has come upon you; and you will be my witnesses *in Jerusalem, in all Judea and Samaria,* and *to the ends of the earth*" (italics added for emphasis).

The first unit of study, "Growing in Strength," deals with passages in Acts 1:1—8:3, which we might call the *witness in Jerusalem* portion of Acts, following the outline in Acts 1:8. As we study how the early church got started, let us ask ourselves how far into the Book of Acts many churches today actually go in practice.

Unit two of this study of Acts is titled "Moving Outward." The Scriptures to be studied are from the *witness in Judea and Samaria* portion of Acts, which is Acts 8:4—12:25. Moving outward was not easy for the early church; it won't be easy for us today.

Unit three is titled "On Mission to the World" and follows Paul and his fellow missionaries as they extended the gospel beyond Jerusalem, Judea, and Samaria. The *witness to all the world* portion of Acts is Act 13:1—28:31. Truly being on mission to the world was risky for the early Christians; it's still risky. Even some fellow Christians in the days of the early church misunderstood what their Christian brothers and sisters were doing as they reached out to the world. Misunderstanding by one's fellow Christians is one of the risks missional churches take.

As we move through much of the Book of Acts in this study, our prime concern is not just to marvel at what Peter did or to learn when Paul was where on which missionary journey. Rather, as we study these Scriptures, we will be looking for what they say to us about our work as a church—what they say about *your* church and what *you* and *your* church need to do. The hope is that this study will help your church move toward becoming a church that is truly a missional church.[6]

Note: The time of the first release of these materials includes Easter. To meet the needs of classes who wish to have a lesson specifically from the Easter Scripture passages at this time, an Easter lesson is included.

UNIT ONE. GROWING IN STRENGTH (ACTS 1:1—8:3)

Lesson 1	Focused on Jesus	Acts 1:1–14
Lesson 2	Empowered to Minister	Acts 2:1–24
Lesson 3	Living in Genuine Christian Community	Acts 2:41–47

NOTES

1. Darrell L. Guder, "Missional Community: Cultivating Communities of the Holy Spirit," *Missional Church: A Vision for the Sending of the Church in North America*, Darrell L. Guder, ed. (Grand Rapids, Michigan: William B. Eerdmans Publishing Company, 1998), 170.
2. Dietrich Bonhoeffer, *The Cost of Discipleship* (New York: The Macmillan Company, 1963; original German edition, 1937), 54.
3. Milfred Minatrea, *Shaped by God's Heart: The Passion and Practices of Missional Churches* (San Francisco: Jossey-Bass, 2004), 11, italics in original.
4. Minatrea, *Shaped by God's Heart*, xvi.
5. Daniel Vestal, *It's Time! . . . an Urgent Call to Christian Mission* (Atlanta, Georgia: Cooperative Baptist Fellowship, 2002), 19.
6. Unless otherwise indicated, all Scripture quotations in "Introduction to the Book of Acts: Toward Being a Missional Church" are from the New Revised Standard Version.
7. Listing a book does not imply full agreement by the writers or BAPTISTWAY PRESS® with all of its comments.

Growing in Strength

To some extent, the history of the church is a generation by generation search for the purpose of the church. Even your congregation's history is an ongoing search to discern the will of God in the midst of the changes that occur in your church and in the larger society.

Some people focus on the church gathered, and the emphasis is on making sure the church is being filled. Their energies are invested in getting people to participate in the "gathering" expressions of being church—attendance, outreach ministries, membership growth, and increasing participation in the varied program structures of church life.

Other people focus on the church scattered, and the emphasis is on making sure the church is involved in the community and world. They invest themselves in being God's people in the world by assuring that the community food pantry is full, making sure the homeless shelter and other such ministries are staffed, and implementing other creative strategies to meet human needs.

Increasing numbers of Christians are beginning to understand the ministry of the church to be an ongoing movement involving both gathering *and* scattering. These folks are discovering the nature and purpose of Christ's church to be *missional.* For them, the church's mission is to continue the ministry of Jesus Christ. The life of Christ's church is to be the incarnational expression of God's heart in the world. The mission of the church's heart is to coincide with the mission of God's heart.

Reviewing the story of the church from the first century on, one can trace ways the Holy Spirit has released transforming creativity and power in the life of the world through the church. However, the church has often filtered the influence of God's Holy Spirit in ways that have impeded the mission of God. Throughout church history, many powers other than Jesus Christ have been the focus of the church.

While many in the history of Christianity have focused on dominion, control, politics, and wealth, at least a remnant has always focused on Jesus Christ. These people thus have scattered to minister to outcasts, feed the hungry, provide water for the thirsty, shelter the homeless, and visit those imprisoned by tyranny. Yet, they have also gathered to worship God in spirit and truth and journey into the depths of prayer, while reaching out to other people to gather with them as well. With Jesus as their focus, they have continued the initiatives of Jesus.

This first unit of study, "Growing in Strength," deals with passages in Acts 1:1—8:3, which we might call the *witness in Jerusalem* portion of Acts, following the outline of Acts 1:8. In these lessons we will see how the early church got started by focusing on Jesus and living accordingly, and we will observe several bedrock practices on which every church needs to take action if it wishes to be a truly missional church.[1]

UNIT ONE. GROWING IN STRENGTH (ACTS 1:1—8:3)

Lesson 1	Focused on Jesus	Acts 1:1–14
Lesson 2	Empowered to Minister	Acts 2:1–24
Lesson 3	Living in Genuine Christian Community	Acts 2:41–47
Lesson 4	Ready to Do Ministry in a New Way	Acts 6:1–7

NOTES

1. Unless otherwise indicated, all Scripture quotations in this unit introduction and lessons 1–4 are from the New International Version.

LESSON ONE

Focused On Jesus

Quick Read

By focusing on Jesus, the church is introduced to significant questions, called to wait for God's gift, offered a new kind of kingdom and power, and motivated to gather constantly in prayer.

Generation by generation, year by year, the church is formed and transformed by the questions we honestly ask and answer. What about your church? What questions are forming and transforming your church today? What is your church learning about the mission of God? How is your church truly focused on Jesus? In fact, how are *you* focused on Jesus? This lesson calls us to consider these questions.

Acts 1:1–14

¹In my former book, Theophilus, I wrote about all that Jesus began to do and to teach ²until the day he was taken up to heaven, after giving instructions through the Holy Spirit to the apostles he had chosen. ³After his suffering, he showed himself to these men and gave many convincing proofs that he was alive. He appeared to them over a period of forty days and spoke about the kingdom of God. ⁴On one occasion, while he was eating with them, he gave them this command: "Do not leave Jerusalem, but wait for the gift my Father promised, which you have heard me speak about. ⁵For John baptized with water, but in a few days you will be baptized with the Holy Spirit."

⁶So when they met together, they asked him, "Lord, are you at this time going to restore the kingdom to Israel?"

⁷He said to them: "It is not for you to know the times or dates the Father has set by his own authority. ⁸But you will receive power when the Holy Spirit comes on you; and you will be my witnesses in Jerusalem, and in all Judea and Samaria, and to the ends of the earth."

⁹After he said this, he was taken up before their very eyes, and a cloud hid him from their sight.

¹⁰They were looking intently up into the sky as he was going, when suddenly two men dressed in white stood beside them. ¹¹"Men of Galilee," they said, "why do you stand here looking into the sky? This same Jesus, who has been taken from you into heaven, will come back in the same way you have seen him go into heaven."

¹²Then they returned to Jerusalem from the hill called the Mount of Olives, a Sabbath day's walk from the city. ¹³When they arrived, they went upstairs to the room where they were staying. Those present were Peter, John, James and Andrew; Philip and Thomas, Bartholomew and Matthew; James son of Alphaeus and Simon the Zealot, and Judas son of James. ¹⁴They all joined together constantly in prayer, along with the women and Mary the mother of Jesus, and with his brothers.

As We Begin This Study

As we begin this study of the Book of Acts, compare Acts 1:1 and Luke 1:1–4. Note that the same person, Theophilus, is addressed in each passage. Too, Acts 1:1 seems to indicate that Acts is the second volume of a two-volume work written by Luke. Based on this understanding that Luke wrote Acts as well as the Gospel of Luke, consider a few basic points about Luke's writing here in Acts.

First, since the Book of Acts is volume two of Luke's two-volume work, the implication is that both the Gospel of Luke and the Book of Acts are well-planned and purposeful. Neither was an afterthought.

Second, Luke was not giving us a day-by-day journal account of the early church. Rather, his intent was to show us snapshots of important moments, events, decisions, people, and principles in the early days of the unfolding movement called Christ's church. In Acts, we see God's Holy Spirit empowering and guiding early believers to break through religious regulations, prejudicial practices, and culturally confining conditions.

Third, the mission of God is the dominant theme in Luke's writing. In the Gospel of Luke, Luke presented Jesus' mission as global in scope and emphasized that there was more to come in fulfilling God's vision. Thus, in the last chapter of Luke and the first chapter of Acts, Jesus told his followers to continue his mission. Jesus was sent to reveal God's mission, and Jesus now sends his disciples to continue God's mission to the farthest reaches of God's creation. The Book of Acts should be read and interpreted as accounts of people sent by Christ to continue his teachings and ministry in the world.

Fourth, Acts offers more than a record of past events. Acts offers the church of the future some footprints, pathways, guide maps, directions, suggestions, clues, and advice for the journey of gathering and scattering according to the guidance of God's Holy Spirit.

As we study the Book of Acts, let us interpret its stories and apply its principles to our life together. We are the apostolic people of God. Let us mature in the missional lifestyle of obedient discipleship to Jesus Christ. Let us learn the implications of God's call on our lives to the end that the divine vision will become more fully realized within us and through our influence in all the world, as we continue the mission of God, ministering as the body of Christ.

Focusing On Jesus Introduces Us to Significant Questions (1:1–2)

Theophilus is addressed in the beginning of both Luke's Gospel and Acts (Luke 1:3; Acts 1:1). We do not know the exact identity of this particular Theophilus. In his Gospel, Luke uses the phrase, "most excellent" (Luke 1:3). This phrase suggests that Theophilus may have held a high official position.

Luke certainly wrote for a wider audience than one man, though. Luke wrote to and for the early church as it was in transition. At the time of Luke's writing, the early church was moving from first generation witnesses of Jesus to a second generation of believers. The church was asking questions such as these: *Who are we? Why are we here? Why did Jesus come? What are the implications of Jesus' coming, ministry, teachings, life, death, and resurrection?*

> . . . The ministry of Jesus' followers is to continue Jesus' ministry as they are empowered by the Holy Spirit.

This believing community, beginning in Jerusalem, originally viewed itself to be a renewal movement within Judaism. They were now beginning to see beyond the boundaries and barriers of this one religious group and nationality. Also, the believing community was no longer focused on reaching only Jewish disciples. Thus, Luke, being a Gentile, saw the need to help these believers catch an understanding of the flow of the Spirit of God, as the church moved beyond its Jewish beginnings.

The early church was reinterpreting itself. The church was searching for clarity and direction in its nature and purpose. In some ways, Luke laid a foundation for this perspective by writing about the central role of the Holy Spirit in the Book of Acts. Even Jesus' words recorded in Luke 24 are now explained to have been offered "through the Holy Spirit" (Acts 1:2). This phrase is a sign of things to come in Acts. For Luke, the ministry of Jesus' followers is to continue Jesus' ministry as they are empowered by the Holy Spirit.

This theme of the Holy Spirit is repeated throughout Luke's Gospel. Luke, more than any other Gospel writer, emphasizes the Holy Spirit in Jesus' ministry. The Holy Spirit is mentioned by messengers sent to Elizabeth and to Mary (Luke 1:15, 35). In Luke 4:1, "Jesus, full of the Holy Spirit, returned from the Jordan and was led by the Spirit in the desert, where for forty days he was tempted." Later,

Jesus' Lordship

The Greek word for *witness* is the same word for *martyr*. As we die to ourselves, we become witnesses of Christ. Through baptism, signifying our death to the old way of life (Romans 6:1–4), we proclaim that we live under the authority of the Lordship of Jesus Christ. Baptism is our external expression of our internal experience. We have committed ourselves to die to our self-centered wills and allow Christ to live in and through us. We fulfill God's purpose for Christ's church as we mature under Christ's authority in our lives.

God's purpose for Christ's church is for Jesus to have authority in the life of each believer as Lord. Baptist New Testament scholar Frank Stagg reminded us, "We are the church when he [Jesus] is present in us, and present in us as Lord."[1]

We cherish our Baptist principles of soul liberty and local church autonomy. But we are not completely free or autonomous. Both our freedom of conscience and our congregational autonomy must be lived within the parameters of Jesus' Lordship in our individual lives and in our life together.

---

when Jesus returned to his hometown and home synagogue, he offered an astounding interpretation of Isaiah 61 concerning "the Spirit of the Lord" (see Luke 4:18–19).

For Luke, the followers of Jesus are to continue Jesus' ministry through the power of God's Holy Spirit. Just as Christ was the visible expression of God, the church becomes the visible witness of Christ, the continuation of his mission. We are to be focused on Jesus.

Focusing on Jesus Calls Us to Wait for God's Gift (1:3–5)

Luke reminded Theophilus of Jesus' post-resurrection appearances. Then, Luke used a wonderful phrase to explain why Jesus appeared to his followers: "he . . . gave many convincing proofs that he was alive" (Acts 1:3). Luke re-connects the readers to Jesus' post-resurrection appearances included in his Gospel: appearing to and disappearing from the Emmaus believers; inviting the disciples to touch him; showing them his hands and feet; and eating in their presence (Luke 24:36–43).

How is your church truly focused on Jesus?

Luke also enumerates the days Jesus appeared among his disciples prior to his ascension. Jesus appeared to them over "a period of forty days" (Acts 1:3). During that time, Jesus taught them about the kingdom of God. Jesus invested forty days among his followers to help them understand the implications of his resurrection. They needed to grasp how the reality of Jesus' resurrection transforms every other reality.

Just as Christ was the visible expression of God, the church becomes the visible witness of Christ, the continuation of his mission.

Luke then emphasized Jesus' instructing his followers to wait in Jerusalem for a baptism with the Holy Spirit (1:5). This approach to life is countercultural. Like us, the disciples were not accustomed to waiting. Humans know how to do, initiate, go, and act. Waiting, though, focuses us on Jesus. If the disciples viewed the continuing ministry of Jesus Christ, the work of the unfolding kingdom of God, to be merely a program to be initiated or a campaign to launch, it would have been spiritually powerless.

The spiritual energy of the church always begins with waiting. Waiting on the Lord is a prerequisite to experiencing spiritual vitality and spiritual power. Humans are spiritually renewed by waiting on the Lord (see Psalms 46:10; 130:5; Isaiah 40:29–31; Romans 8:22–25). The effective ministry of the early church did not depend on a long-range planning process or a strategic plan. The effective ministry of the early church depended on their willingness to wait on the Lord. It still does!

Focusing On Jesus Offers a New Kind of Kingdom and Power (1:6–8)

To be baptized with the Holy Spirit is greater than the water baptism of John the baptizer; to be baptized with the Holy Spirit is to be immersed in the life of the Spirit of God. This baptism with the Holy Spirit is also described in Acts as *poured out* (2:17–18); "given" (5:32; 10:44); *received* (8:15–19); *filled with* (9:17); and *coming on* people (19:6). So the experience of Christ's followers being immersed in the life of the Holy Spirit of God is not so much tied to the *how*, since expressions of the *how* vary, as it is tied to the *why*. The church is immersed in the experience of God's Holy Spirit in order to be

Let us mature in the missional lifestyle of obedient discipleship to Jesus Christ.

The Church Exists By . . .

Theologian Emil Brunner is credited with this powerful statement: "The Church exists by mission as fire exists by burning."[2] What do you think about that statement? Do you agree? If so, how does your life and the life of your church reflect the truth of this image? How is the mission of God evident

- in your perspective on life?
- in your priorities in life?
- in your investments of your resources (time, energy, finances, talents, etc.)?
- in your church's stewardship of funds?
- in your church's programming and emphases?

witnesses of Christ and thus to continue the ministry of Jesus Christ, the incarnation of the mission of God.

One would think that if the resurrected Jesus invested forty days teaching his disciples about the kingdom of God, they would at least have an elementary grasp of its nature and character. However, these disciples were so enthralled with their messianic expectations inherited from the prophetic and rabbinic traditions that they missed the point. Their question as to whether Jesus was going to restore the kingdom to Israel at this time disclosed their

Waiting on the Lord is a prerequisite to experiencing spiritual vitality and spiritual power.

lack of attention in Jesus' *Kingdom of God 101* classes. They were blinded by their doctrines. The disciples' question in 1:6 suggests that it is possible to focus so much on correct doctrine that we miss the mission.

The disciples asked Jesus (1:6), "Lord, are you at this time going to restore the kingdom to Israel?" This question indicates that Jesus' disciples couldn't imagine what God was doing. Too, two thousand years later, we are still just beginning to understand and imagine. Still today, many people fail to grasp Jesus' teachings about the nature and character of the kingdom of God. They focus on politics, nationalism, power, and control. Meanwhile, the kingdom of God continues to refuse these dimensions.

It is significant that Jesus didn't even respond to their question by refining the disciples' view of the kingdom of God. Jesus deflected their question. He spoke to the issue of time, differentiating between *chronos* time and *kairos* time (two Greek words for *time*). *Chronos* time, chrono-logical time, tells us the location of the sun in our hemisphere. *Kairos* time speaks of God's perfect timing. Jesus responded to the disciples' misguided question based on an impoverished concept of God's kingdom by reminding them that God's timing is perfect.

Jesus then offered them a broad strokes concept of just how far the mission of God will reach. The disciples would receive power, but not the variety they expected. It is as if Jesus said, *If it is power you want, power you will receive. But the purpose of God's power is to empower you to be my witnesses in your community, in your region, cross-culturally, and to the ends of the earth.*

God gifts Jesus' followers with the power to be his witnesses. The power of God's Holy Spirit that came on Jesus at his baptism (Luke 3:21–22) is now offered to his followers to continue Jesus' ministry. God does not bestow this power so that Jesus' followers can have power over others. Jesus' power finds its purpose in a basin and towel (see John 13).

Focusing On Jesus Means Gathering Constantly in Prayer (1:9–14)

Jesus' ascension evidently occurred on the Mount of Olives. While Jesus' followers stared into the clouds with their mouths gaping open, "two men dressed in white" reminded them that their feet pointed forward, their knees bent forward, and their eyes were in the front of their heads. Therefore, they needed to move forward. These two messengers also foretold that Jesus would return one day.

> While the Lord is no longer with us in body, he is forever with us in Spirit.

While the Lord is no longer with us in body, he is forever with us in Spirit. So we are not to be preoccupied with Jesus' return. Rather, we are to focus on Jesus—his character and ministry.

Remember, Jesus was a person of prayer. For him, prayer was not a magic bridge between him and the Father. Rather, prayer was an ongoing dialogue between Partners in ministry. Jesus also encouraged his followers to pray. He taught them how to pray. He modeled prayer. He departed to private places for prayer. It is not odd, then, that after Jesus' ascension, his followers "joined together constantly in prayer" (Acts 1:14). When we focus on Jesus, we will join together constantly in prayer.

24

QUESTIONS

1. When a vision is being entrusted to a younger generation by people who are older, what risks are present? What actions can be taken by the older group to assure the vision does not diminish as it is received by the younger group? What actions can the younger group take to assure they are faithful in living out the vision as it is being entrusted to them? How can both groups be renewed in the process of transition, as they re-visit the original vision and re-focus the essence of the vision for a new day?

2. Jesus said he was on earth "to preach good news to the poor . . . to proclaim freedom for the prisoners and recovery of sight for the blind, to release the oppressed, to proclaim the year of the Lord's favor" (Luke 4:18–19). How is your church continuing Jesus' ministry today?

3. The first followers of Jesus—even after hearing his voice, looking on his face, walking with him, and listening to his teachings—did not understand the lifestyle of waiting on the *kairos* timing of the Lord, the Lord's purpose for their lives, or the Lord's vision for the use of power. In what ways are we similar today? In what ways are we different?

4. Even in the midst of confusion and chaos, the earliest followers of Jesus saw the church emerging. What examples can you cite of the church emerging around you today, even amidst the confusion and chaos of our day?

5. Are you involved in a group wherein the primary purpose of the group is prayer? If so, how does this group shape your ministry in the kingdom of God?

NOTES

1. Frank Stagg, *New Testament Theology* (Broadman Press: Nashville, 1962), 266.
2. Emil Brunner, quoted in O.G. Myklebust, *The Study of Missions in Theological Education* (Egede Instituttet: Oslo, Norway, 1955), 27.

Focal Text
Acts 2:1–24

Background
Acts 2:1–40

Main Idea
The Holy Spirit empowers disciples to minister for Jesus.

Question to Explore
Do we rely on our own strength and ignore the Spirit's power?

Study Aim
To describe what happens when people and churches are empowered by the Holy Spirit

Study and Action Emphases
- Affirm the Bible as our authoritative guide for life and ministry
- Share the gospel with all people
- Develop a growing, vibrant faith
- Include all God's family in decision-making and service
- Value all people as created in the image of God
- Obey and serve Jesus by meeting physical, spiritual, and emotional needs
- Equip people for servant leadership

LESSON TWO

Empowered to Minister

Quick Read

For the church to grow stronger, Christ's followers must allow the Lord to lead them, as unlikely witnesses are empowered with new life to proclaim the gospel.

Picture the scene. As Acts 2 begins, we hear birds chirping at the dawn of a new day in the city named Jerusalem. In some ways, this morning is like most other mornings.

Yet, this morning also offers unique experiences. This is the day of Pentecost on the Jewish calendar. Pentecost, the Greek word for *fiftieth*, is the fiftieth day after Passover and the Feast of Unleavened Bread. It is also known in the Old Testament as the Feast of Weeks. It was the time when the first fruits of the wheat harvest were presented as an offering to God. Pentecost was a day of celebration that marks the close of the wheat harvest season, and it also commemorated God's gift of the Ten Commandments to the Hebrews. It was the second of the three greatest festivals of the Jews in Bible times.[1]

This day of Pentecost would itself be unique. Something was about to happen that would make this Pentecost like no other before or since.

Acts 2:1–24

[1]When the day of Pentecost came, they were all together in one place. [2]Suddenly a sound like the blowing of a violent wind came from heaven and filled the whole house where they were sitting. [3]They saw what seemed to be tongues of fire that separated and came to rest on each of them. [4]All of them were filled with the Holy Spirit and began to speak in other tongues as the Spirit enabled them.

[5]Now there were staying in Jerusalem God-fearing Jews from every nation under heaven. [6]When they heard this sound, a crowd came together in bewilderment, because each one heard them speaking in his own language. [7]Utterly amazed, they asked: "Are not all these men who are speaking Galileans? [8]Then how is it that each of us hears them in his own native language? [9]Parthians, Medes and Elamites; residents of Mesopotamia, Judea and Cappadocia, Pontus and Asia, [10]Phrygia and Pamphylia, Egypt and the parts of Libya near Cyrene; visitors from Rome [11](both Jews and converts to Judaism); Cretans and Arabs—we hear them declaring the wonders of God in our own tongues!" [12]Amazed and perplexed, they asked one another, "What does this mean?"

[13]Some, however, made fun of them and said, "They have had too much wine."

[14]Then Peter stood up with the Eleven, raised his voice and addressed the crowd: "Fellow Jews and all of you who live in Jerusalem, let me explain this to you; listen carefully to what I say. [15]These men

are not drunk, as you suppose. It's only nine in the morning! [16]No, this is what was spoken by the prophet Joel:

[17] "'In the last days, God says,
I will pour out my Spirit on all people.
Your sons and daughters will prophesy,
your young men will see visions,
your old men will dream dreams.
[18] Even on my servants, both men and women,
I will pour out my Spirit in those days,
and they will prophesy.
[19] I will show wonders in the heaven above
and signs on the earth below,
blood and fire and billows of smoke.
[20] The sun will be turned to darkness
and the moon to blood
before the coming of the great and glorious day of the Lord.
[21] And everyone who calls
on the name of the Lord will be saved.'

[22]"Men of Israel, listen to this: Jesus of Nazareth was a man accredited by God to you by miracles, wonders and signs, which God did among you through him, as you yourselves know. [23]This man was handed over to you by God's set purpose and foreknowledge; and you, with the help of wicked men, put him to death by nailing him to the cross. [24]But God raised him from the dead, freeing him from the agony of death, because it was impossible for death to keep its hold on him.

All Together Now (2:1)

On this Jerusalem morning, behind serenity and traditional observance another experience was waiting to erupt. It would be a moment to be remembered throughout human history. This was day fifty since Jesus' resurrection from the dead and day ten since Jesus' ascension. The Christ followers were still praying and waiting according to Jesus' command (Acts 1:4, 14). In light of their experiences with the risen Jesus, they must have known that whatever was going to happen next was going to be so important that only God could make it happen. God had brought Jesus back to life and guided Jesus' ascension into the heavens. What was God going to do next?

Why do you think these people continued to pray and expect God to act? Was it obedience? Jesus told them to remain in Jerusalem to pray and wait. By continuing to obey Jesus' command to wait for the gift of the Father, they were focused on Jesus. Were they confident in God's faithfulness? These followers of Christ teach us that prayer is expressing faith in God's faithfulness.

The Church Is Born (2:2–4)

While birds chirped in the foreground, God was working in the background. God was bringing about something new.

God is always in the background bringing about something new. We should not conclude that the disciples' ten-day prayer meeting brought about the miracles of Pentecost. Neither should we think that if we pray fervently for ten days, we too can bring about another experience like Pentecost. Our prayers, though, prepare us to receive the gift of being involved in what God is doing. Like a family gathered outside the delivery room in anticipation, Christ's followers in Acts 2 gathered in expectant prayer, anticipating God was about to birth something new. The day of Pentecost was the day the church was born with the power to continue the ministry of Jesus.

What was God going to do next?

"Suddenly" (2:2), without any advance notice, a sound like the blowing of a violent wind—perhaps like the sound of Hurricane Katrina—came from heaven. This was the first evidence that the Holy Spirit of God was present. The Holy Spirit is associated with the idea of wind in other biblical passages (see 1 Kings 19:11; Ezekiel 37:9).

The first sense of Pentecost was hearing. The second sense of Pentecost was seeing. After hearing this violent wind, Christ's followers saw "what seemed to be tongues of fire" (Acts 2:3). Fire was also used in biblical imagery to represent the presence of God (see Exodus 3:2; 13:21; Isaiah 30:27). Luke records that John the Baptizer foretold this experience: "I baptize you with water. But one more powerful than I will come, the thongs of whose sandals I am not worthy to untie. He will baptize you with the Holy Spirit and with fire" (Luke 3:16).

The Lordship of Jesus Christ always transcends barriers.

These external manifestations of the Holy Spirit—wind and fire—proclaim that spiritual renewal originates with God. Human spiritual leaders cannot generate true spiritual renewal. True spiritual renewal is a work of the Holy Spirit. The power of the Holy Spirit is symbolized by the wind. The fire symbolizes the Holy Spirit to be the abiding presence of God that spreads throughout the world.

After Christ's followers heard the violent wind and saw the fire, the third evidence of the presence of God's Holy Spirit was revealed. Luke reports that "all of them were filled with the Holy Spirit" (Acts 2:4). Each person, male and female, privileged and poor, old and young, immature and mature, follower and leader, is included in this phrase, "all of

> *God was bringing about something new.*

them." The followers of Christ were empowered by the Holy Spirit to speak in unknown languages.

Some people have proposed that the Holy Spirit first came at Pentecost. Yet, according to Luke, this is not the case. Throughout his Gospel, Luke presents the Holy Spirit as an active presence, involved in the lives of Mary (Luke 1:35), Simeon (Luke 2:25–27), and Jesus (Luke 4:1, 14; 10:21).

The Holy Spirit did not show up for the first time at Pentecost. The Pentecost experience was when the Holy Spirit showed up with new power for every follower of Christ. For Luke, the church was born on the day of Pentecost as Christ's followers were empowered to continue the ministry of Jesus.

Empowered to Proclaim the Gospel (2:5–13)

Pentecost was one of the annual festivals that compelled dispersed Jews to return to Jerusalem. Every male Jew living within a twenty-mile radius of Jerusalem was legally bound to attend Pentecost. The festival happened in early June, when weather conditions were excellent for travel. Most likely, more people visited Jerusalem for Pentecost than for Passover, and the crowd was international in character.

Barriers were crossed as people heard the disciples proclaiming the message received from the Holy Spirit. The Lordship of Jesus Christ always transcends barriers.

Acts offers a roll call of those nationalities represented on that day. The Parthians, Medes, Elamites, and the dwellers of Mesopotamia were

Unity Through Diversity

While visiting New York City some years ago, this writer happened on a gathering of thousands, inside a Manhattan cathedral. This gathering involved politicians including the mayor, senators, and the governor. It also involved neighborhood representatives, shopkeepers, educators, business and civic leaders, law enforcement spokespeople, cultural and ethnic group leaders, and gang leaders. They were from every area of the city. They were merging their voices to call for an end to the violence across the city. It was amazing to see and hear the diversity in the voices. At the end of that day, my journal entry included these words: "Lord, I am reminded your kingdom promotes unity through diversity. Today, each of the diverse voices was essential if the audience was going to heed the message and respond with understanding. Thank you for our Baptist heritage that encourages unity through diversity."

from east of Judea. Those from Cappadocia, Pontus, Asia, Phrygia, and Pamphylia represented the many Jews living in Asia Minor. They would have traveled from the Mediterranean coast. Jews had lived in Egypt for more than six hundred years. There were also Jews and converts to Judaism from Rome and Crete. A number of languages would have been spoken by this varied group.

Each year on Pentecost Sunday in our congregation, people who speak languages other than English are enlisted to lead us in reading Acts 2:1–12. To hear this story in Hebrew, Tagalog, German, Arabic, French, Greek, Spanish, African dialects, and Mandarin Chinese is to grasp the experience of Pentecost more clearly. In a time when many Christians are creating barriers and drawing boundary lines, it is important to recall that the church is empowered, by the Holy Spirit, to continue the ministry of Jesus Christ beyond boundaries.

The Pentecost experience was when the Holy Spirit showed up with new power for every follower of Christ.

When Christ's followers remain focused on Jesus, involved in expectant prayer, and open to the inspiration of the Holy Spirit, many people who receive the ministry of Christ are intrigued and want to understand the meaning of the message. There will always be some who mock the moment and confuse inspiration with intoxication, something merely human. This experience of Pentecost, though, cultivated a question within many of the dispersed Jews gathered in Jerusalem. Acts reports their question to be (2:12), "What does this mean?" Their question allowed Peter to offer an explanation.

An Unlikely Witness (Acts 2:14–24)

Enter the room of your imagination. You are part of the second-century church and the only two writings your small community of faith has in its possession are Luke and Acts. You are listening to the story of the emerging church and this experience on the day of Pentecost, when the first sermon shows up in the narrative. The preacher is Simon Peter.

The last time we heard Peter speak in Acts was in Acts 1:15–22. There he was taking care of church administration, replacing Judas with Matthias. Yet, lingering in our memory is how this preacher earlier had proved quite incapable of faithful discipleship. Repeatedly, Peter had denied knowing Jesus (Luke 22:54–62). In Luke's Gospel, there is no story of Peter responding to Jesus' questions, "Do you love me?" with a repetitive *yes* (see John 21:15–19). In Luke's Gospel, we left Peter weeping bitter tears (Luke 22:62). After he ran to the empty tomb, he merely "went away, wondering to himself what had happened" (Luke 24:12). We do have the report in Luke 24:34 of the Lord's appearance to Peter. But we have no direct word from Peter himself. Peter seems an unlikely witness to offer the first sermon by the emerging church.

The promised Messiah has come!

Now, in the twenty-first century, we find tremendous comfort in Peter's sermon. With our compilation of twenty-seven books called the New Testament, we count Peter among the faithful. This sermon is the first of many sermons or speeches in the Book of Acts, most of them by Peter and Paul, another unlikely witness.

The day of Pentecost was the day the church was born with the power to continue the ministry of Jesus.

Peter began his sermon by countering the mockers' assertion of drunkenness (Acts 2:13). Peter pointed out, "It's only nine in the morning" (2:15). The words of these followers of Christ were not proclaimed through inebriation but as a fulfillment of prophecy.

The prophet Joel foretold that during the last days, the days of fulfillment, God would pour out God's Holy Spirit "on all people" (2:17). Some

A Pentecostal Christian?

A coworker accused Sam of not being "a Pentecostal Christian." He suggested the Holy Spirit was not at work in Sam's life. Sam called his pastor. His pastor asked Sam some questions based on Galatians 5:22, as follows;

- Are you expressing love toward others?
- Do you have joy in your life?
- Are you experiencing God's peace?
- Do you patiently wait on the Lord?
- Do you express kindness toward others?
- Are you good to others?
- Are you maturing in faithfulness?
- Do others experience gentleness in you?
- Do you express self-control?

What about you?

---

interpret this phrase to mean all people groups, all nationalities. Others interpret this to be explained by the succeeding clauses: "sons and daughters," "young men," and "old men."

Through twenty centuries of interpretation of Peter's first sermon and his use of Joel's prophecy (Joel 2:28–32), we understand it to mean both.

Still today, God is using unlikely witnesses. . . .

Throughout twenty centuries of church history, women and men, young and old, of all nations, have proclaimed the good news of God, revealed through Jesus Christ. In response, everyone—anyone—of any people group who has called on the Lord has experienced salvation.

The first section of Peter's sermon (Acts 2:22–24) overviewed for the dispersed Jews the man named Jesus. Peter presented Jesus to be a native of Nazareth, a miracle worker, who was put to death on the cross. But, God raised him from the dead. Peter focused on Jesus.

Throughout the remainder of Peter's sermon (2:25–40), he interpreted two passages from the Psalms, Psalm 16:8–11 and Psalm 110:1. It was important for Peter to present Jesus to his Jewish audience as the fulfillment of Jewish Scriptures.

The power emphasized here is not Peter's preaching. The power emphasized is God's. Peter was focused on Jesus. The promised Messiah has come! The prophecies of old are being fulfilled! The last days are here! The age of fulfillment has begun!

Still today, God is using unlikely witnesses—women and men, young and old—to help people understand God's message of hope and salvation. God is empowering the church through the Holy Spirit.

QUESTIONS

1. Consider the meaning packed into Jesus dying at Passover and the Holy Spirit empowering the church on the day of Pentecost. What are some things this would have meant to these early followers of Christ? What does it mean to you?

2. Do you think there is a difference between prayer and expectant prayer? If so, which do you think is more prevalent among today's followers of Christ?

3. Consider the statement, "The day of Pentecost was the day the church was born with the power to continue the ministry of Jesus." Do you agree or disagree?

4. What positive effects do you see of God's pouring out his Spirit "on all people," daughters as well as sons, men and women (Acts 2:17–18)? What concerns do you have?

5. How does your church observe Pentecost Sunday?

6. What difference does it make that the history of the church includes many stories in which unlikely witnesses have been used by God?

NOTES

1. See Exodus 23:14–16; Deuteronomy 16:1–17.

Main Idea

Christians are to live in genuine Christian community—united in learning of Christ, showing love to one another, worshiping God, and including new believers.

Question to Explore

How can genuine Christian community be developed in a world that emphasizes individualism?

Study Aim

To measure the life of our church by the life of the newly begun church in Acts

Study and Action Emphases

- Affirm the Bible as our authoritative guide for life and ministry
- Share the gospel with all people
- Develop a growing, vibrant faith
- Include all God's family in decision-making and service
- Value all people as created in the image of God
- Obey and serve Jesus by meeting physical, spiritual, and emotional needs
- Equip people for servant leadership

LESSON THREE

Living in Genuine Christian Community

Quick Read

Each believer contributes to or subtracts from a congregation's capacity to experience genuine Christian community.

The pastoral candidate stepped to the pulpit for the "trial sermon." The pastor search committee had developed a profile of those characteristics they sought in their next pastor. They had prayed, sifted through scores of résumés, prayed, checked references, prayed, pursued interviews and finally, through prayer, settled on this candidate to present to the congregation "in view of a call." The pastoral candidate now uttered the first words the congregation would hear their new pastor say from the pulpit: "For the next few minutes, you and I will be involved in similar explorations. You are exploring whether I can preach a good sermon. I will explore whether you know one when you hear one!"

Acts 2:41–47

41Those who accepted his message were baptized, and about three thousand were added to their number that day.
42They devoted themselves to the apostles' teaching and to the fellowship, to the breaking of bread and to prayer. **43**Everyone was filled with awe, and many wonders and miraculous signs were done by the apostles. **44**All the believers were together and had everything in common. **45**Selling their possessions and goods, they gave to anyone as he had need. **46**Every day they continued to meet together in the temple courts. They broke bread in their homes and ate together with glad and sincere hearts, **47**praising God and enjoying the favor of all the people. And the Lord added to their number daily those who were being saved.

More Than Numbers (2:41)

For some people, a good sermon results in converts to Christian discipleship. If this is the criterion for an effective sermon, Peter's first sermon was highly effective. He had preached it on the day of Pentecost after Christ's followers were empowered by the Holy Spirit to continue the ministry of Jesus. Thousands of people responded to Peter's sermon. Or did they? Did they respond to Peter's sermon, or did they respond to the gospel of Christ?

The passage of Scripture we are considering in this study begins and ends with the numerical growth of the church. Verse 41 refers to approximately 3,000 Jews who responded to Peter's sermon and were baptized, becoming Christ's followers, on the day of Pentecost. These individuals—the audience of dispersed Jews described in Acts 2:5–11—represented diverse nations, customs, and languages. The response can be described as instantaneous church growth.

At the end of the study passage, Acts 2:47 offers this summary, "And the Lord added to their number daily those who were being saved." This verse refers to Jerusalem Jews who were becoming Christ's followers through their day-to-day encounter with the life of the Holy Spirit at work in the early believers. They were drawn into the community of faith through watching and experiencing how the followers of Christ loved one another.

Did they respond to Peter's sermon, or did they respond to the gospel of Christ?

These references to numbers point beyond themselves. They were evidence that the life of the Spirit was being embraced by more and more people. The events of the day of Pentecost started about 9:00 A.M. (see Acts 2:15) with a few people experiencing the empowerment of the Holy Spirit. By day's end, thousands had entered the waters of baptism and the life of discipleship to Christ. What was going on in the early church was much more than numerical growth; it was genuine Christian community.

On Being the Church (2:42–47a)

Today, we use the word *church* to describe a local body of believers. We also use the word to refer to all those baptized believers throughout history, in all parts of the earth, who make up the membership of Christ's body of disciples. When we talk about church in the latter sense, the wider sense, many images come to the forefront of our minds—relationships, traditions, people, doctrines, programs, experiences, principles, institutions, heritage, family, friends, music, sermons, windows, architecture, and so on.

However, before us, before our parents and grandparents and their parents, before any denomination or doctrine, what was the church? How did it get started, and what was included?

It is to this subject that Acts now takes us. Acts has told us about Jesus' ascension, the gathered believers selecting a replacement for Judas, the Holy Spirit empowering Christ's followers on the day of Pentecost, the message of Jesus being understood in a variety of languages, and Peter's sermon resulting in 3,000 converts in one day. Now, Acts begins to tell of incidents that defined the nature and functions of the early church.

Remember, Luke was writing to second-generation believers. By the time Luke's readers came across his words, the early Christian movement was already being called *the church* and consisted primarily of Gentiles.

Yet, Luke began his description of the early church as beginning in Jerusalem and consisting primarily of Jews. Much had changed over the intervening decades, perhaps sixty or so years.

> *They were drawn into the community of faith through watching and experiencing how the followers of Christ loved one another.*

The first thing Acts tells us is that these first followers of Christ "devoted" themselves to some common practices (Acts 2:42). The word "devoted" means to *give your self fully to*. They did not just vote about these practices in a business meeting or go through the motions or dabble. They gave themselves fully to "the apostles' teaching and to the fellowship, to the breaking of bread and to prayer" (2:42). In addition, they were all "filled with awe" (2:43); "were together" (2:44); "had everything in common" (2:44); shared their resources to meet one another's needs (2:45); met together daily (2:46); participated in the Lord's Supper (2:46); had fellowship around meals (2:46); participated in worship (2:47); and enjoyed a favorable reputation among the citizens of Jerusalem (2:47). Each of these experiential realities was a dimension of genuine Christian community. Consider several of them in detail, especially those mentioned in Acts 2:42.

By devoting themselves to "the apostles' teaching," the early followers of Christ were united in their desire to learn of Jesus. They were devoted to a study of the apostles' recollections of Jesus' teachings and lifestyle principles as well as to the apostles' interpretations of Hebrew Scripture and theology in the light of Christ.

> *. . . Too often we treat the church as though it belongs to us and thus is to be controlled by us.*

It is significant that the early church realized the importance of establishing a solid theological and scriptural foundation for their commitment to Christ. If their movement had simply been an emotional response to the departure of their leader or a weekly reenactment of an emotional frenzy on the day of Pentecost, they would have followed quite a different path.

Living as a Genuine Christian Community

Prepare to contribute to the conversation in your church that will encourage your church in living as a genuine Christian community. In addition to studying and applying this series of Bible study lessons, encourage your pastor, pastoral staff, and core church leaders in moving your church in this direction. One practical and helpful book on this topic is by Baptist author Milfred Minatrea. The bibliographical information is as follows: Milfred Minatrea, *Shaped by God's Heart: The Passion and Practices of Missional Churches* (San Francisco: Jossey-Bass, 2004).

The apostles were seeking to understand how Christ fulfilled Hebrew Scripture. For Luke, the Scriptures of the Jews put the life of Jesus in context. The apostles did not focus on *Christianizing* the Hebrew Scriptures. Rather, they sought to help people understand how Jesus fulfilled them. The apostles were diligent in discovering how Jesus was the answer to God's promises. These early followers of Christ "devoted themselves to the apostles' teaching" (2:42).

When we allow the life of faith in community to fulfill God's intention . . . church becomes something mysterious and powerful.

The early followers of Christ also devoted themselves to fellowship. From the outset, they responded to Jesus' command, offered during the Last Supper, "Love each other" (John 15:17; see 13:35). Their expressions of love for each other engendered and nurtured the experience of *koinonia*, a Greek word referring to fellowship based on vulnerability, authenticity, mutual humility, and honesty.

They also regularly observed the Lord's Supper. This was another way Christ's followers kept their focus on Jesus. In Jewish tradition, when the blessing is offered for the meal, the table and the shared meal become sacred. This tradition would have been solidly entrenched in the observances of these early disciples. These early believers understood that worship involves more than one hour a week. Worship is a lifestyle.

Luke considered their devotion to prayer to be noteworthy, too. Possibly, they observed prayers at the hours established in Jewish tradition. They did continue to meet daily in the courts of the temple (2:46). Jesus had taught the disciples to pray (Luke 11:1). By continuing to give themselves fully to prayer, these early Christians continued to focus on Jesus.

41

The Early Church and Today's Church (2:47b)

Today, many churches across America search to rediscover the essence of church. Too often, churches really do not desire spiritual renewal, though. Rather they desire institutional survival or organizational success. Most churches make attempts toward spiritual renewal by reaching out for the latest idea. They should be reaching within for a new depth of relationship between themselves and the Spirit of God. However, most reach out for better electronics and technology or experiences tilted in the direction of entertainment aimed at gathering a crowd. Some churches even buy into the modern corporate mindset to the extent that marketing strategies are viewed to be the recipe for renewal.

Their sense of awe in relation to God motivated their devotion to learn of Christ, to love one another, to worship, to pray, and to include new people in the faith community.

If, however, a church truly wants to rediscover the DNA, the essence, of the Jesus movement, it must focus on the values that produce genuine Christian community, especially these:

- Learning of Christ—studying the life of Christ, especially through studying Scripture and interpreting it by Christ[1]
- Loving one another—growing in relationships based on vulnerability, honesty, authenticity, and mutual humility that move beyond individualism to relational faith
- Worshiping God—focusing on the sacrificial life and teachings of Jesus Christ and his discipline of prayer as dialogue with God about God's desire and vision for the church and the world
- Including new believers—extending warm hospitality that embraces diversity and assimilates new people into the life of the faith community

As local churches pursue these core values, they will live as genuine Christian communities. However, too often we treat the church as though it belongs to us and thus is to be controlled by us. When we allow the life of faith in community to fulfill God's intention, though, church becomes something mysterious and powerful.

As these words are being written, a nineteen-year-old United States Marine is being mourned in our church. People are reaching out to his parents and young sister to express compassion and ministry. He was killed by a bomb in Iraq, after being deployed for only three weeks. He had trained for eighteen months and was pursuing his dream. In the midst of his parents' immense grief, they cannot say enough about the thoroughness of the genuine love they are receiving from the church. Neighbors have mentioned they have never seen such love. The church, though, is merely being the church.

Genuine Christian community begins to emerge when a church believes in the gospel of Christ to the extent that it makes a decisive difference at the center of individual and communal Christian faith. Genuine Christian community begins to emerge when a church expresses a deep compassion for people and people groups whose lives are in disarray because they do not or cannot rely on God.

Acts has enriched our understanding of the essence of the church by reviewing the characteristics and pursuits of the early followers of Christ. Yet, it must be said that Bible study and theological inquiry do not make us the church. Relating to one another through vulnerability, authenticity, and mutual humility does not make us the church. Gathering for worship each week does not make us the church. Too, prayer does not make us the church. So, what is it that makes us the church?

Genuine Christian community begins to emerge when a church believes in the gospel of Christ to the extent that it makes a decisive difference at the center of individual and communal Christian faith.

Acts offers us these words: "Everyone was filled with awe" (2:43). I believe it was their awe of God that motivated the involvements of these early followers of Christ. Their sense of awe in relation to God motivated their devotion to learn of Christ, to love one another, to worship, to pray, and to include new people in the faith community. Their awe of God transformed their relationships into realms beyond human dimensions. It was their awe of God that made them the church.

What is "awe"? "Awe" is the word you say after you consider all the wonders of God's creation—all the grace, all the mercy, all the love, all the justice that flows from God's hand; and all the ways God's providence has worked to reveal God's nature and will to us. As you think of all this and more, your jaw drops and the word-sound you make is "awe."

You can contribute to the process of church renewal. Pray and become devoted. Pray for God's vision for your church. Too, pray that you, your household, and your Bible study group will be devoted to God's vision for your church. Further, as a person and as a class, become devoted to learning the teachings and lifestyle principles of Jesus Christ; to loving one another; to living a lifestyle of worship; and to including others in the life of the church. Yet, above all, in all, and through it all guard your worship; guard your awe of God!

QUESTIONS

1. What is the impact of the following on a church's spiritual health? What would you say are the top five in producing spiritual health?

    a. Preaching

    b. Worship

    c. Teaching

    d. Music style

    e. Openness to new people

    f. Marketing

    g. Sense of awe

    h. Prayer

    i. Love for one another

2. What images come to your mind when someone asks you about the church? How can we help people outside the church understand that church is so much more than a building or a gathering?

3. What example comes to mind about when you experienced genuine Christian community?

4. How devoted is your church to

- Learning of Christ?

- Loving one another?

- Worshiping God?

- Including new believers?

NOTES

1. As the 1963 *Baptist Faith and Message* states, "The criterion by which the Bible is to be interpreted is Jesus Christ."

Focal Text
Acts 6:1–7

Background
Acts 6:1–7

Main Idea
Churches that effectively meet needs are open to doing ministry in new ways.

Question to Explore
Why do we get stuck in doing ministry the same old ways when new situations call for new approaches?

Study Aim
To describe why and how the early church developed a new approach for ministry and draw parallels to new ministry opportunities today

Study and Action Emphases
- Affirm the Bible as our authoritative guide for life and ministry
- Develop a growing, vibrant faith
- Include all God's family in decision-making and service
- Value all people as created in the image of God
- Obey and serve Jesus by meeting physical, spiritual, and emotional needs
- Equip people for servant leadership

LESSON FOUR

Ready to Do Ministry in a New Way

Quick Read
Missional churches are always searching for opportunities to initiate new ministries, even when needs are disguised as conflict situations.

We are fortunate to be living in one of the most exciting times in the history of humanity. A friend recently observed, "If I hadn't been born in this period of time, I would have bought a ticket to travel to our here and now."

In May 2006, I participated in a trip to Kenya, Zambia, Zimbabwe, and Botswana, for a two-week immersion in the life situation of Africa's poor. In the shade of a small banana grove, in the remote village of Chinyanya, Zambia, while eating lunch with a farmer and his family, miles from electricity, with no indoor plumbing, our conversation was interrupted by the ring of a cell phone.

We are living in an amazing period of time. Walls of distance and separation are being eliminated by communication technologies. Travel limitations are being erased by aerodynamics, and language barriers are being diminished by computerized programs.

Like the earliest followers of Christ, we are confronted with new opportunities and challenges. If we are to live in the world as God's missional church, we must be ready to do ministry in new ways. We are stewards of the church's ministry in the world. This is both a tremendous blessing and a challenge.

Acts 6:1–7

[1]In those days when the number of disciples was increasing, the Grecian Jews among them complained against the Hebraic Jews because their widows were being overlooked in the daily distribution of food. [2]So the Twelve gathered all the disciples together and said, "It would not be right for us to neglect the ministry of the word of God in order to wait on tables. [3]Brothers, choose seven men from among you who are known to be full of the Spirit and wisdom. We will turn this responsibility over to them [4]and will give our attention to prayer and the ministry of the word."

[5]This proposal pleased the whole group. They chose Stephen, a man full of faith and of the Holy Spirit; also Philip, Procorus, Nicanor, Timon, Parmenas, and Nicolas from Antioch, a convert to Judaism. [6]They presented these men to the apostles, who prayed and laid their hands on them.

[7]So the word of God spread. The number of disciples in Jerusalem increased rapidly, and a large number of priests became obedient to the faith.

Where Genuine Christian Community Takes Us (Acts 3—5)

In our last study, we focused on Acts 2:41–47. We considered the values that produce genuine Christian community: learning of Christ; loving one another; worshiping God; and including new believers.

This session's study focuses our attention on Acts 6:1–7. What happened in Acts 3—5? What paths did this genuine Christian community take on its way to Acts 6?

First, genuine Christian community guided Peter and John to minister to a crippled man on their way to prayer in the temple (Acts 3:1–10). Their ministry to this man opened the door for Peter to proclaim the resurrection power of Jesus Christ (3:11–26). Their explanation resulted in the priests and temple guards seizing them and placing them in jail overnight. However, many who heard them believed their message and decided to follow Jesus (4:1–21).

We are fortunate to be living in one of the most exciting times in the history of humanity.

Second, this experience of Peter and John emboldened the other believers. These Christ followers embraced the sovereignty of God at a new level of depth and boldness (4:22–31).

Third, the believers became more united than ever before; they became "one in heart and mind" (4:32). Possessions were shared, not hoarded. Believers shared their testimony of life with Jesus Christ. Needy people among them were cared for by the sacrifices of others. Barnabas surfaced as a leader among the early church because of his commitment to this way of Christian community and because of the ways in which his faithfulness encouraged others (4:32–37).

Fourth, those who sought to live pretentiously, in the presence of this genuine community, such as Ananias and Sapphira, became object lessons for others (5:1–11).

Fifth, miraculous signs resulted in the continued growth and ministry of the church (5:12–42).

Thus, we learn that the pathway of genuine Christian community always focuses on Jesus Christ; exhibits boldness and courage in the face of religious corruption and challenge; engenders trust and sacrifice over pretense and selfishness; and expresses faithfulness in the face of threat and political power. This pathway brings us to the experience of a church growing in numbers and in diversity and confronts us with challenges.

The Church as Steward of Ministry Opportunities (6:1)

The first challenge to genuine Christian community arose out of church growth and cultural pluralism (6:1). This should not surprise us. One of the most significant subjects of our conversation these days has to do with cultural pluralism. Border guards do not exist only between nations. Border guards are present in many congregations. These border guards sort through Sunday's guests to determine who should be invited to return.

Many people focus the witness of the church on moral issues and nothing else. Certainly, the church must be clear as to the teachings of Scripture on topics such as poverty, crime, violence, war, abortion, sexuality, capital punishment, social and economic relationships, and so on. However, while these moral values must be addressed, the issues that truly threaten the witness of Christ's church must not be overlooked.

The witness of Christ's church in today's world is most threatened by inauthentic fellowship, shallow discipleship, and artificial worship. The witness of Christ's church is threatened every time those who are supposed to focus on the life of Christ within them turn their backs on Christ to split a congregation over carpet color, property location, or music style. The witness of Christ's church is threatened each time mean-spiritedness controls people who should be peacemakers; each time greed overpowers the poor; each time we choose inciting discord over controlling oneself; each time we choose selfish ambition over faithfulness; and each time we invest our energies in dissension rather than in gentleness and sacrifice.

If we are to live in the world as God's missional church, we must be ready to do ministry in new ways.

We can learn from the old cartoon character, Pogo, who reported to his commander, after a long night of blind shooting between their platoon and other soldiers. Pogo went to scout out the position of those firing at their platoon and returned with these words: "Sir, we have met the enemy, and they are us."[1] Under the cover of darkness, the platoon had been shooting at one another.

It is possible for Christ's church to get caught up in political causes, trying to vote candidates into office who support legislation of one party over another, and completely abandon the mission of God for Christ's church. Most likely, many Christians will continue to debate one another over ethical and moral perspectives and political positions, firing at one another under the cover of darkness. However, we must learn to see one another through the light of the gospel, not as citizens of a nation, but as citizens of God's kingdom. Otherwise, Pogo's words will continue to come true: "We have met the enemy, and they are us."

If Christ's church is to embrace a missional identity, we must move beyond a moralistic and political focus. Rather we must view ourselves as stewards of ministry opportunities. We must refuse to sacrifice our missional calling on the altar of any person, group, organization, or institution that requires our allegiance and obeisance. Our Lord is Jesus Christ; we need no other. Let us be willing to work *with* anyone toward the vision of God's kingdom, while refusing to work *for* anyone who demands we pay them homage. Let us be stewards of ministry opportunities, ever ready to do ministry in ways outside the cultural limitations of the past. The earliest followers of Christ can help us learn this lesson.

> *Like the earliest followers of Christ, we are confronted with new opportunities and challenges.*

Discovering Ministry Opportunities in the Midst of Conflict (6:2–4)

Luke tells us the root of this conflict: "the number of disciples was increasing" (6:1). We have traveled 178 verses deep into the story of the early

---

Church Autonomy and the Priesthood of Believers

Baptists embrace the principles of the autonomy of the local church and the priesthood of each believer. These principles have been both neglected and attacked in recent years. This study of Acts 6:1–7 reminds us that each Baptist congregation must express autonomy under the Lordship of Jesus Christ, as stewards of the mission of God. In addition, each congregational member is competent under God to express faith without having to submit to some person wielding positional power. ✳

Congregational autonomy and the priesthood of believers may bring conflict into the life of the church. Yet, without these principles embraced by Baptists throughout our history, church becomes an institutionalized organization, void of spiritual power and insensitive to people who are being overlooked.

church to find their unity to be under siege. Numerical church growth and cultural diversity blended to create the problem. This should not surprise us.

Numerical church growth creates many issues that are often hidden. The rapid increase in numbers of possible relationships contributes to potential conflict. When only two people are in a group, there are only two possible relationships—*A* with *B* and *B* with *A*. When three people are in a group, there are six possible relationships—*A* with *B*, *A* with *C*, *B* with *A*, *B* with *C*, *C* with *A*, and *C* with *B*. The mathematical formula for determining the number of possible relationships is $PR=N^2-N$. *PR* represents *possible relationships in the group*. *N* represents the number of people in the group. If your group has twelve people, you have 132 possible relationships in your group ($132 = 12^2$ [144] − 12). Now, consider your congregational membership. If your church has 300 members, you have 89,700 possible relationships in your church. If your church has 1,500 members, you have 2,248,500 possible relationships among the membership.

> We must refuse to sacrifice our missional calling on the altar of any person, group, organization, or institution that requires our allegiance and obeisance.

In Acts 2:41, Luke tells us about 3,000 responded to Peter's sermon at Pentecost. But, these people were from many nations. Acts 2:47 mentions that people were being added to the church daily. Acts 4:4 tells us the number of men grew to about 5,000. So, by the time we get to Acts 6:1, the number of people involved in the Jerusalem church was at least 5,000. This would mean this early group of Christ's followers was trying to tend to at least 24,995,000 possible relationships. No wonder they had conflict!

> Let us be stewards of ministry opportunities, ever ready to do ministry in ways outside the cultural limitations of the past.

The other issue at the root of this conflict had to do with cultural diversity. It can be difficult trying to sustain congregational harmony with Baylor Bears, Texas Longhorns, and A&M Aggies or with Auburn Tigers and Alabama Crimson Tide fans among the congregants. (Fine-tune this reference by inserting the names of the leading college athletic teams from your own locale.) Just imagine how difficult it would be to nurture harmony among a group of whining Grecian Jews whose widows were being overlooked by a group of inattentive Hebraic Jews. Getting red states and blue states to cooperate is nothing new.

At this early point in development, the church consisted of Jews only. The Grecian Jews had been born in nations other than Palestine. They spoke the Greek language, which was the language of the Roman Empire, and they had more of a Greek than Hebrew perspective about life. The Hebraic Jews spoke Aramaic or Hebrew, the historic languages of Palestine, and they focused on preserving Jewish customs and culture. In other words, the *Alabama* widows were being neglected by *Auburn* fans in the daily distribution of "Meals on Wheels" (please substitute whatever are the greatest rivalries in your area).

> *Whatever challenge or conflict your congregation may experience, look for ministry opportunities, especially those disguised as conflict.*

This story includes so much more than conflict, though. This is a story about ministry opportunities disguised as conflict. When you listen closely, you may find that people who voice their feelings of being neglected are voicing a legitimate concern.

Rather than creating a codependent system in which they were controlled or manipulated, the apostles stayed focused on their primary calling to guide the people in prayer, worship, teaching, and proclamation. The people did not say to the apostles, *We have a problem, and we want you to own it, solve it, and give it back to us fixed.* Rather the apostles offered an idea, and the people received it well.

The apostles asked the people to select seven men from among them to address this issue. The men chosen needed a reputation of relying on the Holy Spirit and expressing wisdom.

Although Acts does not use the term *deacon* here, some suggest these seven were the first deacons in the life of the church. While this may or may not be true, this account certainly offers insight into the essence of being a deacon—being a servant.

The passage also reveals some significant truths about the life and ministry of the church. First, the life and ministry of the church calls for leadership. Spiritual leadership is not threatened by delegating responsibility to people who rely on the Holy Spirit and use wisdom in making judgments. Second, the congregation was open to choosing leaders to help them minister in new ways. A need was identified, and a ministry group was chosen to alleviate the need. Third, leadership arises from below and is not handed down from above. The ministry of the church, for the health and life of the church, is *by* the church.

Case Study

Janie and Sam dropped out of church life after her mother died. They moved Janie's mother into their home during her last months with cancer. Patsy saw Janie in the grocery store and asked whether the church had failed them in some way. Janie thanked Patsy for asking and then said, "While Mama was dying, nobody from the church called, sent a note, or came by to visit us. We were out of church for sixteen months. We thought someone would contact us, but it never happened. We are now looking for another church."

If you were Patsy, what would you do?

Doing Church in New Ways (6:5–7)

An amazing reality rises out of this story. Each man chosen, all seven, were Grecian Jews. Listen to their names: Stephen, Philip, Procurus, Nicanor, Timon, Parmenas, and Nicholas. Each is a Greek name. The Hebraic Jews allowed the Grecian Jews to be the first servant leaders chosen by the early church to minister in new ways. Territorialism took a back seat to servant leadership for the good of the body of Christ. The early church needed something done and devised a means of getting it done.

This story may seem a little out of place in between imprisonments and martyrdom in Acts. Yet, this story represents a foundational truth of the church's life. The witness of the church and the power of the church are not threatened most by outside influences. The witness and power of the church are threatened most by those who focus more on problems and conflicts than they do on becoming part of the solution.

Ministering in new ways is more important than who gets the credit.

These seven men became so much more than caregivers of the widows. Their willingness to be servants behind the scenes, their dependence on the Holy Spirit, and their wisdom engendered their emergence onto the more public stage of church leadership. Acts 7—8 tells how Stephen and Philip were used greatly in open proclamation of the gospel in the early days of Christ's church.

Acts 6:7 overviews the result of being willing to do church in new ways: "The word of God spread. The number of disciples increased rapidly, and a large number of priests became obedient to the faith." The church, when open to doing church in new ways, finds a power otherwise unknown.

Whatever challenge or conflict your congregation may experience, look for ministry opportunities, especially those disguised as conflict. Encourage the pastor and other spiritual leaders to join you in prayer as you pursue a new approach to ministry. Too, let us all learn this lesson from the early church in Acts: *Ministering in new ways is more important than who gets the credit.*

QUESTIONS

1. What opportunities for ministry does your church have today that were unavailable twenty years ago?

2. Who are the people who would not be welcomed into the life and ministry of your congregation? Why? How do you feel about this? How does your congregation communicate a lack of welcome and acceptance to these people? What can your church do to solve this problem?

3. What does a church forfeit if it becomes more involved in politics and policing society's morals than in the mission of God?

4. How does your church tend to the many needs represented by your membership? How do you make sure no one is neglected by your church's ministry?

5. How are leaders chosen in your church? What expectations of leaders does your church embrace that qualify a person for spiritual leadership?

6. Who are some of the most effective and influential spiritual leaders you have known? What made these people effective and influential as spiritual leaders?

NOTES

1. Comic strip "Pogo," by Walt Kelly.

Moving Outward

This unit, "Moving Outward," deals with the way God worked among the first-century disciples to carry the gospel beyond Judaism and Jerusalem to the Gentile world. The Scriptures to be studied are from what many Bible students consider the *witness in Judea and Samaria* portion of Acts (see Acts 1:8), which is Acts 8:4—12:25. The passages show how the early church began to move beyond simply sharing the gospel with Jews and insisting that people become Jews if they wanted to become Christians. These first-century disciples began to share the gospel with Gentiles as well as Jews.

Immediately before the first of the passages to be studied in this unit, the laity in the church in Jerusalem had been scattered through persecution (see Acts 8:1–3, especially 8:1b). These lay Christians began sharing their faith wherever they went. ✳

As a result, in these lessons, we will travel with Philip into Samaria, where he witnessed a great awakening, and then to Gaza, where he was God's instrument in the conversion of the treasurer of Ethiopia. We will witness the remarkable conversion of the chief persecutor of Christians, Saul of Tarsus, who became Paul the Apostle. Saul was one of the least likely Christian converts of all time, and yet he came to be included in the Christian community. We will look at how this happened. We will travel with Peter and visit a Gentile home in Caesarea Philippi. There God redefined all preconceived ideas about who is acceptable in his sight. Then, we will journey to Antioch and witness the early beginnings of a new church that God would use to launch the gospel to the ends of the earth.

In this unit we will learn (1) how God desires to move *us* beyond our comfort zones in serving him; (2) how God wants *us* to include the least likely; (3) how God *still* wants to overcome all barriers that stand in the way of people coming to faith; and (4) how God wants to use *us* to reach out to all people. If we learn the lessons the early disciples learned in these chapters of Acts, we will never be the same.[1]

NOTES

1. Unless otherwise indicated, all Scripture quotations in this unit introduction and lessons 5–8 are from the New American Standard Bible (1995 edition).

Background
Acts 8:1–40

Main Idea
God calls us to reach out to people our culture may reject.

Question to Explore
Who are the people beyond your church's comfort zone whom God is calling your church to reach?

Study Aim
To summarize how early Christians began to reach out to people beyond their comfort zone and identify people beyond our church's comfort zone whom God is calling our church to reach

Study and Action Emphases
- Affirm the Bible as our authoritative guide for life and ministry
- Share the gospel with all people
- Develop a growing, vibrant faith
- Value all people as created in the image of God
- Obey and serve Jesus by meeting physical, spiritual, and emotional needs
- Equip people for servant leadership

LESSON FIVE

Reaching Beyond the Comfort Zone

Quick Read
As we follow Philip into Samaria and then to Gaza, we learn how God calls us beyond our comfort zones to reach people our culture may reject.

More than thirty years ago, Martin Luther King, Jr., said that 11 A.M. to noon on Sunday is the most segregated hour of the week in America.[1] Still today, most Christians attend churches with people who look like them, speak like them, dress like them, and act like them. It is a comfortable hour in a comfortable place.

The early disciples felt much the same. They were comfortable in Jerusalem after Jesus' resurrection. The number of disciples was growing daily (Acts 2:47). But the church was mono-cultural. Only Jews were included. The apostles appear to have had no plan to extend the gospel outside Jerusalem. This thought may sound shocking at first, but it makes perfect sense when we consider that they expected Jesus' final return at any moment and did not understand God's plan to redeem people of every culture, language, and nation. This they would have to learn.

Most of us start out in the same way. We find ourselves in a comfortable fellowship of believers. We do not realize that God desires to push us beyond our comfort zone to places and people we do not know.

God allowed the early church to suffer persecution in order to move them into new regions and cultures. Stephen, one of the seven laymen selected in Acts 6, was stoned to death following his bold witness before the high priest (Acts 7). This event started a widespread persecution of the church in Jerusalem so that the believers were scattered throughout Judea and Samaria (8:1b). As a result, these who were scattered began sharing the good news of Jesus with people of different cultures. They were catapulted outside their comfort zone and saw God do amazing things.

Acts 8:4–8, 14–17, 26–36

⁴Therefore, those who had been scattered went about preaching the word. ⁵Philip went down to the city of Samaria and began proclaiming Christ to them. ⁶The crowds with one accord were giving attention to what was said by Philip, as they heard and saw the signs which he was performing. ⁷For in the case of many who had unclean spirits, they were coming out of them shouting with a loud voice; and many who had been paralyzed and lame were healed. ⁸So there was much rejoicing in that city.

. . . .

¹⁴Now when the apostles in Jerusalem heard that Samaria had received the word of God, they sent them Peter and John, ¹⁵who came down and

prayed for them that they might receive the Holy Spirit. **¹⁶**For He had not yet fallen upon any of them; they had simply been baptized in the name of the Lord Jesus. **¹⁷**Then they began laying their hands on them, and they were receiving the Holy Spirit.

. . . .

²⁶But an angel of the Lord spoke to Philip saying, "Get up and go south to the road that descends from Jerusalem to Gaza." (This is a desert road.) **²⁷**So he got up and went; and there was an Ethiopian eunuch, a court official of Candace, queen of the Ethiopians, who was in charge of all her treasure; and he had come to Jerusalem to worship, **²⁸**and he was returning and sitting in his chariot, and was reading the prophet Isaiah. **²⁹**Then the Spirit said to Philip, "Go up and join this chariot." **³⁰**Philip ran up and heard him reading Isaiah the prophet, and said, "Do you understand what you are reading?" **³¹**And he said, "Well, how could I, unless someone guides me?" And he invited Philip to come up and sit with him. **³²**Now the passage of Scripture which he was reading was this:

"He was led as a sheep to slaughter;

And as a lamb before its shearer is silent,

So He does not open His mouth.

³³ "In humiliation His judgment was taken away;

Who will relate His generation?

For His life is removed from the earth."

³⁴The eunuch answered Philip and said, "Please tell me, of whom does the prophet say this? Of himself or of someone else?" **³⁵**Then Philip opened his mouth, and beginning from this Scripture he preached Jesus to him. **³⁶**As they went along the road they came to some water; and the eunuch said, "Look! Water! What prevents me from being baptized?"

God Pushes Us Beyond Our Comfort Zone: Reaching People Unlike Ourselves (8:4–8)

Acts 8 describes Philip's journey into Samaria. Samaria was a region shunned by the Jews. Samaria was located between the northern region of Galilee and the southern region of Judea. Most Jews went out of their way to avoid crossing through Samaria. They wanted nothing to do with the Samaritans.

Samaritans were a racially mixed population. Many of the ruling class and gifted craftsmen had been carried away in captivity centuries before this time. After the northern region of Israel fell to Assyria in 722 B.C., the peasants and rabble were left behind. They intermarried with the Gentile foreigners whom the Assyrians then settled there (see 2 Kings 17:18–24). Consequently, the Jews of Jerusalem despised the Samaritans as inferior half-Jews. Jesus broke this stereotype by traveling through Samaria (John 4:3–5), by visiting with a Samaritan woman (John 4:7–42), and by making a Samaritan one of the best-known characters in his parables (Luke 10:30–37).

> Today every continent touches every other continent.

Philip had been selected along with Stephen in Acts 6:1–6 to serve the church. Philip found himself in the same region that Jesus visited. When he told the Samaritans about Jesus' crucifixion and resurrection, they immediately responded with faith. It is as if they had been waiting for someone to tell them. Philip had crossed the barrier of culture to reach people unlike himself.

Think about what has happened in the last few years. September 11, 2001 stands out in our minds as a watershed moment in American history. Our world changed forever the moment the first silver-bodied jet crashed into the Twin Towers. The horror of the hours that followed was forever written in our minds and captured on videotape. Contrary to much popular opinion, however, that moment did not mark the

Which Philip?

As in our day, different people in New Testament times often shared the same name. The Philip who appears in these passages is not to be confused with Philip from Bethsaida, one of the twelve disciples of Jesus (Matthew 10:3; John 1:43–51; 6:5–7; 12:21–22; 14:8–9). Neither is the Philip of Acts to be confused with Philip the brother of Herod (Luke 3:1–2; Matt. 14:3).

The Philip who is featured in Acts 8 first appears in Acts 6:1–6. He is one of the seven men chosen by the church to minister to the widows because he was "of good reputation, full of the Spirit and of wisdom" (Acts 6:3). After carrying the gospel into Samaria and after his journey into Gaza, he was led by the Spirit northward to Azotus, about twenty miles north of Gaza. He continued his northward journey until he settled in Caesarea. There he appears to have married and raised a family. Luke records that he and Paul visited Philip in Caesarea about twenty years later and makes note of his four daughters who were "prophetesses" (21:8–9).

beginning of terrorism. Terrorism already existed. We just realized for the first time that the security we had felt was gone. We were no longer a nation in relative isolation, guarded and protected by the Atlantic and Pacific. The world had shrunk.

Today every continent touches every other continent. Every nation rubs up against every other nation. Every culture spills over into every other culture.

I first met Khalil Jaloub in 2004 and was fascinated with his story. Khalil was born in Baghdad and grew up a Muslim. He left Iraq to study in England and then the United States. Disillusioned with Islam, he decided to explore other religions. He wandered into a Baptist church in Oklahoma. For the first time he heard about God's love and God's provision for salvation through Jesus. He

. . . God desires to push us beyond our comfort zone to places and people we do not know.

became a believer and married a Christian. As I am writing this lesson, Khalil is the minister of missions at a church in Plano, Texas. God is moving millions of people like Khalil all around the world.

In every city and in many towns and communities, we are near people who are different from us. More than 100 different languages are now spoken in Houston. More than 47 million people in the United States (about 16% of the population) speak a language other than English at home. That includes 28 million people who speak Spanish at home, more than 2 million who speak Chinese at home, 1 million who speak Vietnamese, and about 900,000 who speak Korean.[2] Detroit is home to one of the largest concentrations of Arabs outside the Middle East.

The movement of population groups around the earth is creating unprecedented opportunities to share the gospel and demonstrate the love of Christ.

To some, this increasingly diverse ethnic population in the United States creates cause for alarm. The old comfort zones and securities are being challenged. But to the eye of the believer, God is at work. The movement of population groups around the earth is creating unprecedented opportunities to share the gospel and demonstrate the love of Christ. ✶

The Ethnic America Network was founded to connect more than sixty evangelical denominations and agencies in the United States in order to reach more effectively the first and second generation immigrants to America. Our churches no longer have to travel to the other side of the earth to engage the mission field. For those willing to step outside their comfort zone, missions is at the door.

God Pushes Us Beyond Our Comfort Zone: Laity Taking the Lead (8:4–8)

Those who first carried the gospel outside Jerusalem were the laity. Acts 8:1 states that as a result of the persecution "they were all scattered throughout the regions of Judea and Samaria, *except the apostles*" (italics added for emphasis). Acts 8:4 further states that "those who had been scattered went about preaching the word." Clearly, the apostles stayed in Jerusalem while the laity carried the message to Judea and Samaria.

The apostles, of course, are the Twelve. They would have hardly thought of themselves as clergy. They were fishermen, tax collectors, and businessmen whom Jesus collected from the lakes, hills, and villages of Galilee. (Only Judas was from Judea.) But they were the closest thing to clergy the church had at this early stage.

Later, beginning in the early centuries of the church, Christendom became comfortable with the clergy-laity dichotomy. The clergy became the religious professionals. They were comfortable with the authority and influence given them by their position. Laity became comfortable with menial tasks around the church. They could pray for the professional

How to Apply This Lesson

- Study the demographics of your community. What ethnicities are represented?
- Drive through your community looking at the different stores and other businesses. What ethnic groups are represented?
- Visit with someone this week who is of a different ethnicity or culture from your own.
- Look for ethnic churches in your community. Contact one or more of these churches and visit one of their services.
- Pray for God to lead you to someone who is open and seeking to know him.
- Volunteer for a mission trip to another country.

missionaries, give their offerings, and support the professional clergy. Until recently, it has been a relatively comfortable arrangement.

But God is once again pushing believers beyond their comfort zone. God wants all of God's people empowered and equipped to do all of God's work. When the laity realize this truth and seek to respond to God's calling, tension is sometimes created with an unwilling clergy who feel threatened. When the clergy realize this truth and seek to equip and deploy the laity for ministry, the clergy are sometimes frustrated by an unwilling laity who prefer the comfortable shadows of religion relegated to Sunday mornings and minimal commitment.

In the twenty-first century we are witnessing a movement of the laity for missions unprecedented since the first century. God is at work among God's people. The connected world and global economy are creating opportunities for Christian lay men and women to take their passion and their professions to the ends of the earth. People who have skills in medicine, technology, education, and business can go almost anywhere on earth and

> *We must be willing to step outside our comfort zone of religion, where we control everything.*

share the gospel. Instead of a few thousand professional missionaries, God desires to send hundreds of thousands of his people to share the gospel.[3] God is teaching us once again the beauty of God's church in which pastors are the equippers and the laity are equipped "for the work of service" (Ephesians 4:11).

God Pushes Us Beyond Our Comfort Zone: Letting God Take Control (8:14–17)

Most of what we do as churches is predictable. We have adopted the latest business models for promotion, marketing, development, and organization. In many of our churches, little takes place that cannot be explained in term of business practices. Even our evangelistic efforts are often built on sales techniques.

We are always more comfortable when we are in control. But what happens when God takes control?

When Philip entered Samaria (Acts 8:4–8), he could not have predicted what would happen. Many were healed, and others were delivered from evil spirits. Many were baptized (8:12). When Peter and John arrived to see what was happening, they prayed for the believers and laid hands on them so that they might receive the Holy Spirit.

The fact that the Samaritans had been baptized in the name of Jesus but had not received the Holy Spirit may appear confusing. Being baptized in the name of Jesus and receiving the Holy Spirit is the difference between identifying with a religion and entering into a personal relationship with Jesus Christ by faith. The actions of Simon (8:9–24) indicate that many of these Samaritans were responding to the miracles and being baptized without fully understanding a faith relationship with Jesus.

We must be willing to step outside our comfort zone of religion, where we control everything. We must be willing to step into the uncomfortable position where God is in control and we are filled with the Holy Spirit.

God Pushes Us Beyond Our Comfort Zone: Letting God Take Us to Places That Are God's Choice Rather Than Ours (8:26–36)

I am sometimes amazed at how we approach missions on the basis of convenience. My wife and I are native Texans. When God called us to minister in Minnesota in 1993, many of our friends wondered in amazement that we would move a thousand miles away where winters lasted six months and temperatures plunged to 55 degrees below zero. I would often tell them I could not find the Scripture where God said, *So send I you to favorable climates not too far from home.*

God spoke to Philip and told him to go south to the desert road leading to Gaza. When Philip arrived, he met a court official of Ethiopia. He was a eunuch who was returning from Jerusalem. The eunuch could have been a Jew or a God-fearer. A God-fearer worshiped the God of Israel but was not fully a Jew. Likely he was a Jew, either by birth or as a proselyte. Even if he was a Jew, however, he would not have been considered a fully acceptable Jew if he was a physical eunuch. A physical eunuch would not have been fully accepted as a Jew, whether by birth or as a proselyte (Deuteronomy 23:1). At any rate, he was examining the Scripture and reading Isaiah 53, the messianic prophecy foreshadowing Jesus' crucifixion.

God still sends his people to specific places at specific moments.

66

Philip obeyed the Spirit's instruction to go to the eunuch's chariot and speak to him. Philip heard the eunuch reading Isaiah's prophecy. Philip engaged the eunuch in conversation. Philip then accepted the eunuch's invitation to explain what the Scripture meant. Philip "preached Jesus to him," telling him that God had fulfilled this prophecy in Jesus (Acts 8:35). If Philip had not listened to God and obeyed God's instruction, he would not have been there to lead this influential Ethiopian to Christ.

God still sends his people to specific places at specific moments. In 2004, Heather Herschap called WorldconneX, which connects "people, churches, entities and resources for missions." She said, "I am a student at Truett Seminary and I have cerebral palsy. God has called me to India. How can you help me?" I drove to Waco and visited with Heather. Although she is confined to a wheelchair, has limited use of one arm, and has a speech impediment, Heather is one of the most radiant Christians I have ever met. She said she was in church in Waco, Texas, and God whispered in her hear, "India." Through connections we were able to make with ProVision Asia, Heather went to India in 2005 to work with people with disabilities.

We seldom experience God in the comfortable places.

When I went to Minnesota I met Chuck Friemel. Chuck had been an air traffic controller until he was laid off work. He used the setback to discover God's plan for his life. He enrolled in seminary and prepared himself as a church planter. When Chuck came to visit Minnesota, the director of missions told him he could show him a number of places where he could plant a church. Chuck said he was willing to look at any place the director wanted to show him, "But," he said, "God has called me to Red Wing." Chuck moved to Red Wing, Minnesota, in 1991. He took a job in a local ice skate factory to make a living while he started the Hiawatha Valley Baptist Church in Red Wing. As of this writing, Chuck is now the longest tenured pastor in the city.

Just as God sent Philip to Samaria, Heather to India, and Chuck to Red Wing, God can send you to people and places you never imagined. We seldom experience God in the comfortable places. When we follow God outside our comfort zones we discover God's glory, God's power, God's presence, and God's pleasure. God is always faithful when we trust in him.

QUESTIONS

1. How does the ethnic makeup of your church compare to the ethnic makeup of the public schools in your community?

2. Where do you most often interact with people of another ethnicity or culture?

3. What can clergy do that laity cannot do?

4. Has God ever directed you to a particular person or a particular place? When and how did God do this?

NOTES

1. Martin Luther King, Jr. "Remaining Awake Through a Great Revolution." Delivered at the National Cathedral, Washington, D.C., on March 31, 1968. See www.africanamericans.com/MLKRemainingAwakeThrough GreatRevolution.htm. Accessed 10/5/2006.
2. "Language Use and English-Speaking Ability: 2000," Census Brief from the United States Census Bureau.
3. William Tinsley, *Finding God's Vision: Missions and the New Realities* (Rockwall, TX: Veritas Publishing, 2005), available at www.veritaspublish.com.

4-29-07

Focal Text
Acts 9:10–28

Background
Acts 9:1–31

Main Idea
A church following Christ needs to find ways to include outsiders, even the least likely, in its fellowship.

Question to Explore
How effective—really—is your church in including "outsiders" in your fellowship?

Study Aim
To describe how Saul, Christianity's fiercest opponent, came to be included in the Christian community and to consider how we can include "outsiders" in our fellowship

Study and Action Emphases
- Affirm the Bible as our authoritative guide for life and ministry
- Share the gospel with all people
- Develop a growing, vibrant faith
- Include all God's family in decision-making and service
- Value all people as created in the image of God
- Obey and serve Jesus by meeting physical, spiritual, and emotional needs
- Equip people for servant leadership

LESSON SIX
Including the Least Likely

Quick Read
This lesson examines how the early disciples included the least likely convert so that their greatest adversary became their strongest leader. Today, too, a church following Christ must find ways to include outsiders, even the least likely.

I sat across the table from Ahmed[1] and listened to his story. Ahmed was born in Istanbul. He grew up there in a prosperous and devout Muslim family. As a youth he was zealous for Allah. In fact, as a young man he was sent to an eastern European country to win converts to Islam. All he knew of Christianity came from Islam and his exposure to Hollywood films. To Ahmed, Christianity represented immorality, materialism, greed, and corruption.

Ahmed enrolled in a university in Eastern Europe. There he met Lori,[2] a young woman from Texas serving on a two-year mission assignment. She was working in the university library. She invited Ahmed to Bible studies in her apartment and gave him his first Bible. She was the first authentic Christian he had ever met, and the Bible she gave him was the first Bible he had ever read. Ahmed came to faith in Jesus Christ.

When Ahmed's family learned of his conversion, he was ostracized and targeted for persecution. Ahmed escaped to the United States. There Lori's parents adopted him as their son. Now thirty-two, Ahmed was about to graduate with a Ph.D. from a university in Texas. He visited with me at WorldconneX to discover how he could return to the Muslim world as a witness for Christ.

Ahmed has much in common with Saul of Tarsus, a young man who started out opposing Christ and became a dedicated believer. What would have happened to Saul and to Ahmed if someone had not believed in each of them and included them?

Acts 9:10–28

[10]Now there was a disciple at Damascus named Ananias; and the Lord said to him in a vision, "Ananias." And he said, "Here I am, Lord." [11]And the Lord said to him, "Get up and go to the street called Straight, and inquire at the house of Judas for a man from Tarsus named Saul, for he is praying, [12]and he has seen in a vision a man named Ananias come in and lay his hands on him, so that he might regain his sight." [13]But Ananias answered, "Lord, I have heard from many about this man, how much harm he did to Your saints at Jerusalem; [14]and here he has authority from the chief priests to bind all who call on Your name." [15]But the Lord said to him, "Go, for he is a chosen instrument of Mine, to bear My name before the Gentiles and kings and the sons of Israel; [16]for I will show him how much he must suffer for My name's sake." [17]So Ananias departed

and entered the house, and after laying his hands on him said, "Brother Saul, the Lord Jesus, who appeared to you on the road by which you were coming, has sent me so that you may regain your sight and be filled with the Holy Spirit." ¹⁸And immediately there fell from his eyes something like scales, and he regained his sight, and he got up and was baptized; ¹⁹and he took food and was strengthened.

Now for several days he was with the disciples who were at Damascus, ²⁰and immediately he began to proclaim Jesus in the synagogues, saying, "He is the Son of God." ²¹All those hearing him continued to be amazed, and were saying, "Is this not he who in Jerusalem destroyed those who called on this name, and who had come here for the purpose of bringing them bound before the chief priests?" ²²But Saul kept increasing in strength and confounding the Jews who lived at Damascus by proving that this Jesus is the Christ.

²³When many days had elapsed, the Jews plotted together to do away with him, ²⁴but their plot became known to Saul. They were also watching the gates day and night so that they might put him to death; ²⁵but his disciples took him by night and let him down through an opening in the wall, lowering him in a large basket.

²⁶When he came to Jerusalem, he was trying to associate with the disciples; but they were all afraid of him, not believing that he was a disciple. ²⁷But Barnabas took hold of him and brought him to the apostles and described to them how he had seen the Lord on the road, and that He had talked to him, and how at Damascus he had spoken out boldly in the name of Jesus. ²⁸And he was with them, moving about freely in Jerusalem, speaking out boldly in the name of the Lord.

Including Others Requires Risk (9:10–12)

If anyone ever represented a risk to the Christian community, it was Saul of Tarsus. By his own admission, he was ambitious (Philippians 3:2–6; Galatians 1:13–14). Born into privilege, he was both a Roman citizen and a Jew by birth. He had received the best education available, having been tutored personally by Gamaliel, the most famous teacher in Jerusalem (Acts 22:3). He was a zealous Pharisee, rapidly advancing in political and religious power among his peers (Gal. 1:13–14). He had been present at Stephen's death, holding the coats of those who stoned him (Acts 7:58). Afterward, he became an aggressive leader in the persecution at Jerusalem that caused the believers to scatter for safety (8:1; 9:1). Fueled by his success, Saul requested and received warrants for the arrest of Christians in Damascus and set out on a personal mission to search out and destroy the followers of Christ.

Saul left Jerusalem as an ambitious and angry young man, probably in his late twenties or early thirties. He arrived in Damascus blind and confused. On the way, he had met the resurrected Jesus face to face and heard him speak. Struck to the ground by a blinding light, Paul lost his sight and had to be led by the hand into the city (9:1–9).

When Paul arrived in Damascus, he was taken to a specific house on Straight Street. There he waited in darkness, surely praying that someone would help him understand what had happened to him.

We must ask ourselves whether we are being obedient to Jesus' voice in our generation.

Damascus was an ancient city. In fact, it may well be the oldest continuously inhabited city in the world. Located approximately sixty miles northeast of the Sea of Galilee, it flourished as a crossroads of commerce, linking trade routes to Egypt, Arabia, and Mesopotamia. The sights, sounds, and smells of the bazaars of Damascus continue today, perhaps much as they were when Saul of Tarsus arrived there. The street where Saul found lodging and prayed for help is still there.

The Lord spoke to a disciple in Damascus named Ananias. We know nothing else about Ananias. He is not to be confused with the other Ananias who lied to the Holy Spirit along with his wife Sapphira and fell dead (5:1–6). This Ananias was apparently one of the believers who had escaped the persecution in Jerusalem and sought refuge in Damascus.

. . . When we follow Christ in believer's baptism, we not only identify with Jesus, proclaiming our personal faith in him, but we also identify with all those who have followed Jesus.

The Lord specifically instructed Ananias to visit Saul of Tarsus and talk to him regarding the gospel and God's plan for his life. The stakes for Ananias could not have been higher. Instead of hiding from the lead persecutor of Christians, he had been instructed to seek him out and witness to him.

What might have happened if Ananias had refused to take a chance on Saul of Tarsus, who later became known as Paul the Apostle? We might never have had the Book of Acts or the Letters of Paul that form two-thirds of the New Testament.

What would have happened to Ahmed if Lori had not included this Muslim missionary in her personal Bible study? What if her family had not adopted him? What difference might Ahmed make in the future witness to Muslim communities around the world?

Including Others Requires Discernment (9:13)

We are not to conclude that willingness to take risks to include others implies that we are to be gullible or naïve. Risk must be tempered with discernment. Notice that the Lord did not reproach Ananias for being cautious. Ananias was fully aware of Saul's activity before he went to meet him. Ananias accepted the risk with open eyes.

Including someone does not mean they are to be placed immediately in positions of leadership and entrusted with responsibility. Influence must be earned. Saul of Tarsus did not immediately become Paul the Apostle. His transition to leadership and influence took many years.

By his own account, Paul left Damascus for Arabia and three years later went up to Jerusalem. There he visited with Peter for more than two weeks and met with James, Jesus' half-brother (Gal. 1:13–24). Afterward he went to his hometown of Tarsus in Cilicia. There Barnabas found him and recruited him to help in the church at Antioch (Acts 11:19–26). Later, after a full year serving as a Bible study leader, Saul was commissioned to accompany Barnabas on the first missionary journey (13:1–3). Paul himself later counseled his young protégé Timothy regarding new converts with these words: "An overseer, then, must be above reproach . . . not a new convert, so that he will not become conceited . . ." (1 Timothy 3:2–6).

Lottie Moon

One of the best-known names among Baptists is Lottie Moon. Commissioned in 1873 to serve as a missionary to China, Charlotte (Lottie) Moon died on Christmas Eve in 1912 after giving her last savings away to feed her starving Chinese friends.

Baptists who grew up studying WMU missions materials know these things. What most people don't know is that Charlotte Moon was fiercely opposed to the gospel during her youth. As a teenager, she would have been considered one of the least likely people, not only to become a Christian, but also to become the namesake for missions since the nineteenth century.

Including Others Requires Obedience (9:14–17)

We could wish we were always motivated by compassion and love. But the fact of the human experience is that we most often love those who love us, those we already know, and those who are easy to love. We cannot rely on our emotions in order to love the stranger, the alien, or our adversary. Such love requires obedience (Matthew 5:46–47).

Encouragement is a constant element in the work of God.

Ananias did not risk his life to visit Saul because he felt great compassion for the persecutor who had recently arrived from Jerusalem. His only motivation was obedience to the voice of God. When Jesus instructed Ananias to seek out Saul to comfort and counsel him, Ananias had no other choice but to go if he was to be obedient. As a disciple, he had already made the decision to obey whatever God told him to do.

Such obedience, of course, is the mark of being a disciple of Jesus Christ. Being a disciple of Jesus Christ means being willing to do whatever Jesus tells us to do. Jesus' mother summed up the responsibility of a disciple when she gave instruction to the servants at the wedding feast of Cana: "Whatever He says to you, do it" (John 2:5). Jesus highlighted obedience as the secret to being his disciple when he said, "Go therefore and make disciples . . . teaching them to observe all that I have commanded you. . . " (Matt. 28:19–20). We tend to focus on knowledge. Jesus focused on action: "Teaching them to *observe*" (italics added for emphasis).

We must ask ourselves whether we are being obedient to Jesus' voice in our generation. Most of those who have never heard the gospel live within Muslim, Hindu, and Buddhist territories. Most of these are within what is called *the 10/40 window*, stretching from West Africa across Asia (10 degrees to 40 degrees north of the equator). Only about 2.5% of the mission workforce is assigned to these regions.

As followers of Jesus Christ, we must look constantly for ways to include the outsider in our fellowship.

The remaining 97.5% of the mission workforce are assigned to areas where the gospel is already available.[3] Are we obediently including these billions of people who have been excluded from a gospel witness?

What about the Muslim, Hindu, and Buddhist communities in our own cities? Are we making any effort to tell them about Jesus?

74

Including Others Requires Encouragement (9:18–28)

What Saul of Tarsus needed now was encouragement and counsel. None of the people who came with him to Damascus could help him. Who would believe him? Who would help him?

A blind Saul sat in darkness in a solitary room on Straight Street in Damascus, refusing to eat or drink (Acts 9:9). In a vision, he saw a stranger named Ananias who would help him. When Ananias arrived, he needed no introduction. Saul was waiting expectantly for him.

We probably don't have the full account of the conversation between Ananias and Saul. But we do have some key elements of what happened. Ananias laid his hands on Saul. There is nothing magical about laying hands on another person, for religious or even Christian purposes. But there is something special. When Saul felt Ananias's hands touch him, he felt the touch of acceptance. Touching and embracing are the universal symbols of acceptance and inclusion.

> *Being a disciple of Jesus Christ means being willing to do whatever Jesus tells us to do.*

Doubtless Ananias bore witness to Saul regarding Jesus, explained to him the importance of the Holy Spirit, and told him about the destiny God had for him. Ananias's encouragement through word, touch, and presence was far more important to Saul than his physical sight. In fact, the Bible indicates that for the rest of Saul's life, he may have suffered from problems with his sight (see Gal. 4:15; 6:11; 2 Corinthians 12:7–9).

Immediately, like the Ethiopian official, Saul was baptized. Baptism is a significant symbol by which we identify with Jesus. Many people today

How to Apply This Lesson

- Write down the names of three or more people you consider the least likely to become believers in Christ. Pray daily for these.
- Look for opportunities to encourage others. Keep an "encouragement" journal in which you list the encouragements you are able to give to others each day.
- Think of someone in your circle of contacts (at work, at school, in your neighborhood) who is most opposed to the gospel. How can you befriend this person? How can you show God's love to him or her?

discount baptism as unnecessary and insignificant. But when we follow Christ in believer's baptism, we not only identify with Jesus, proclaiming our personal faith in him, but we also identify with all those who have followed Jesus. Obviously, to the first-century followers of Christ, baptism was important. Baptism symbolizes our acceptance into relationship with God and relationship with fellow believers. By baptizing Saul, Ananias became Saul's gateway to the community of believers.

But Saul was not so readily accepted in Jerusalem. When he arrived in Jerusalem, the followers of Christ were skeptical and suspicious. They wanted nothing to do with the widely known leader of the persecution that had resulted in the death and imprisonment of their family and friends. But Barnabas was willing to take a chance.

> *God is at work in the life of every human being, even those we think to be enemies of the gospel.*

Barnabas emerges as one of the pivotal figures in the early church, simply because he had a gift for encouraging and believing in people. His name literally means *son of encouragement* or *son of exhortation*. He was otherwise known as Joses or Joseph. He was a Levite from the island of Cyprus who had sold his land and given the money to the early church (Acts 4:36–37). It may be that the name Barnabas was given to him because of his consistent gift of encouragement.

Barnabas was willing to risk his reputation (and his life) on this well-known enemy of the church who claimed to be a convert. Barnabas believed anyone could change and anyone should be given a chance. Barnabas stood up for Saul and introduced him to the apostles.

The phrase "took hold of him" is significant in that it indicated the level of Barnabas's commitment to Saul (4:27). The Greek word used here (*epilambano*) is the same word used in Matthew 14:31 when Peter was sinking in the sea and Jesus "took hold of him" by the hand. It is also used in 1 Timothy 6:12 to describe how the believer is to "take hold" of eternal life. The decision by Barnabas to encourage Saul was one of deep commitment.

This idea is reflected further in the fact that some time later Barnabas was the one who brought Saul to Antioch (Acts 11:25–26). Barnabas had been sent to Antioch to examine the reported growth of the church. There Gentiles were coming to faith and were being accepted into the church. When he discovered the powerful evidence of God's work at Antioch, he immediately thought of Saul. Barnabas traveled personally to Cyprus to find him. As a result of Barnabas's action, he and Saul were launched on the first missionary journey (13:1–3). Without Barnabas the encourager, we might never have known Paul the Apostle.

Encouragement is a constant element in the work of God. In fact, the term in the Gospel of John for the Holy Spirit (*paraklete*; see John 14:16) means *exhorter, comforter,* or *encourager.* God is always speaking words of encouragement to his people. The Adversary, on the other hand, is constantly whispering words of discouragement and despair. One of the major responsibilities of the Christian community is to encourage one another. "Not forsaking our own assembling together . . . but encouraging one another" (Hebrews 10:25).

> *The redemption story is always the story of God including the least likely, even us, into his family.*

As followers of Jesus Christ, we must look constantly for ways to include the outsider in our fellowship. God is at work in the life of every human being, even those we think to be enemies of the gospel. The redemption story is always the story of God including the least likely, even us, into his family.

QUESTIONS

1. How many of the new members who have joined your church in the last three years are still active in your church?

2. When you became a Christian, who was most instrumental in encouraging, counseling, and including you in the life of the church?

3. How does your church provide follow-up activities and counseling to new converts?

4. How does your church include (or assimilate) new members into the life of the church?

NOTES

1. Name has been changed for security reasons.
2. Name has been changed for security reasons.
3. Ralph D. Winter and Bruce A. Koch, "Finishing the Task," in Ralph D. Winter and Steven C. Hawthorne, eds., *Perspectives on the World Christian Movement* (Pasadena, California: William Carey Library, 2000), 519.

Focal Text

Acts 11:1–18

Background

Acts 10:1—11:18

Main Idea

Missional churches follow God's leadership when God challenges them to break barriers that stand between them and full participation in God's mission to reach all people.

Question to Explore

What barriers keep your church from doing all that God wants you to do?

Study Aim

To identify barriers God is challenging our church to break in order to participate fully in God's mission to reach all people

Study and Action Emphases

- Affirm the Bible as our authoritative guide for life and ministry
- Share the gospel with all people
- Develop a growing, vibrant faith
- Include all God's family in decision-making and service
- Value all people as created in the image of God
- Obey and serve Jesus by meeting physical, spiritual, and emotional needs
- Equip people for servant leadership

LESSON SEVEN

Breaking Barriers

Quick Read

God led Peter to cross racial and cultural barriers to reach all people. We will learn how churches can overcome barriers in order to become truly missional.

"I have your book [meaning the Bible]," the Muslim man said, "and for two years I have been reading it. I have been crying out to God for someone to come and explain it to me." He said these startling words to four young men who were on a trip to the Middle East with Mary Carpenter, professor of Cross-Cultural Missions at Howard Payne University in Brownwood, Texas. Mary and her group of students had been walking down the streets visiting the shops and bazaars of the city when the man invited the young men into his home for tea. For the next four hours, the students answered his questions.

Mary and her companions experienced a powerful demonstration of God at work opening the heart of a man from a different culture and religion on the other side of the earth. They would never have witnessed God's faithfulness if they had not crossed the barriers that separated them.

The account of Peter's experience with Cornelius in Ceasarea is perhaps the most pivotal passage in the Book of Acts. Note that our focal text, Acts 11:1–18, is Peter's summary of what had occurred in Acts 10. Up until this time the followers of Christ had continued to assume that only those who were Jews could be saved. They continued to hold to this notion in spite of what had happened with Philip and the Samaritans and the Ethiopian court official in Acts 8. God exploded Peter's preconceived ideas about Gentiles, though, through the vision on the housetop in Joppa and the subsequent visit to Cornelius's home in Caesarea. This story became the deciding factor at the Jerusalem council (Acts 15:1–21). As a result, the first-century church came to embrace people of every language, culture, and nation who demonstrated repentance and faith in Jesus Christ alone for salvation.

What can we learn from Peter's experience that will help us understand and overcome the barriers that keep our churches from reaching all people in the twenty-first century?

Our Greatest Barriers Are Within Us

I occasionally visit with people and churches who assume they cannot engage in missions because of external circumstances. Most often, they cite the lack of money. They say they simply can't afford it. Interestingly, the lack of money never appeared to be a barrier to the first-century church. Too, just as interestingly, even today often those who have the least are the ones who are doing the most in missions.

Acts 11:1–18

[1]Now the apostles and the brethren who were throughout Judea heard that the Gentiles also had received the word of God. [2]And when Peter came up to Jerusalem, those who were circumcised took issue with him, [3]saying, "You went to uncircumcised men and ate with them." [4]But Peter began speaking and proceeded to explain to them in orderly sequence, saying, [5]"I was in the city of Joppa praying; and in a trance I saw a vision, an object coming down like a great sheet lowered by four corners from the sky; and it came right down to me, [6]and when I had fixed my gaze on it and was observing it I saw the four-footed animals of the earth and the wild beasts and the crawling creatures and the birds of the air. [7]"I also heard a voice saying to me, 'Get up, Peter; kill and eat.' [8]"But I said, 'By no means, Lord, for nothing unholy or unclean has ever entered my mouth.' [9]"But a voice from heaven answered a second time, 'What God has cleansed, no longer consider unholy.' [10]"This happened three times, and everything was drawn back up into the sky. [11]"And behold, at that moment three men appeared at the house in which we were staying, having been sent to me from Caesarea. [12]"The Spirit told me to go with them without misgivings. These six brethren also went with me and we entered the man's house. [13]"And he reported to us how he had seen the angel standing in his house, and saying, 'Send to Joppa and have Simon, who is also called Peter, brought here; [14]and he will speak words to you by which you will be saved, you and all your household.' [15]"And as I began to speak, the Holy Spirit fell upon them just as He did upon us at the beginning. [16]"And I remembered the word of the Lord, how He used to say, 'John baptized with water, but you will be baptized with the Holy Spirit.' [17]"Therefore if God gave to them the same gift as He gave to us also after believing in the Lord Jesus Christ, who was I that I could stand in God's way?" [18]When they heard this, they quieted down and glorified God, saying, "Well then, God has granted to the Gentiles also the repentance that leads to life."

We often think that external circumstances and conditions prevent us from reaching all people, but this is seldom true. First-century Christians were faced by numerous obstacles that could have prevented them from carrying the gospel to every nation. They were often persecuted. Travel was unpredictable, dangerous, and difficult. They had little money. None of these things proved to be barriers that could prevent them from obeying the Great Commission. But there were other barriers that were much more difficult to overcome. These were the barriers from within.

Our Traditions Create Barriers to Doing All God Wants Us to Do

Peter's vision and experience challenged his long held Jewish traditions. As a devout Jew, he had always been careful to maintain the dietary traditions of his ancestors. All of his close personal relationships had been confined to other Jews like himself. But his faith in Jesus Christ challenged all these assumptions.

Jesus clearly stated that one of the great barriers that prevented people from following him was their traditions (Mark 7:1–8). Paul confessed that his zeal for his traditions was one of the reasons he persecuted the followers of Christ (Galatians 1:13–14).

Traditions in and of themselves are not wrong. In fact, our traditions often enrich and guide our lives. Paul exhorted the Thessalonian Christians to ". . . stand firm and hold to the traditions which you were taught. . . " (2 Thessalonians 2:15). But when we allow our traditions to blind us to the work of God to redeem all people everywhere, these traditions become a barrier and a stumbling block. It's been said that the seven last words of the typical Baptist church are, *We never did it that way before.* Like Tevye, the father in the musical *Fiddler on the Roof* who had to deal with challenges to tradition by new ideas, we often struggle to keep our footing while trying to balance our traditions against a rapidly changing world.

It's been said that the seven last words of the typical Baptist church are, We never did it that way before.

Our Prejudice Creates Barriers to Doing All God Wants Us to Do

When Peter visited Cornelius, he had to overcome the prejudice that could have prevented him from entering a Gentile's home. That this was a significant issue for Peter is reflected in his statement to Cornelius and Cornelius's friends when he said, "You yourselves know how unlawful it is for a man who is a Jew to associate with a foreigner or to visit him; and yet God has shown me that I should not call any man unholy or unclean" (Acts 10:28).

Most of us are blind to our own prejudices. But when we encounter others who look, dress, and speak differently, we are prone to make generalizations based on our preconceived opinions. Unless we consciously work at it, we will not be able to overcome the barriers of prejudice that keep us from seeing other people as individuals.

Our Lack of Prayer Creates Barriers to Doing All God Wants Us to Do

When God gave the vision to Peter on the housetop in Joppa, Peter was engaged in prayer. We don't know how long he had been praying, but we do know he went up on the roof to pray about the sixth hour, or noon (10:9). If Peter had not been praying, he would not have seen the vision. Had he not seen the vision, he would not have gone with the messengers to Caesarea, and the gospel might have remained trapped within the Jewish culture and traditions. Prayer was the key that opened up the possibilities for God to intervene.

> *Most of us are blind to our own prejudices.*

Acts 10:1–6 gives us some essential information about Cornelius. Cornelius was a centurion in command of an Italian cohort. This means he was a Gentile Roman officer. Typically centurions commanded one hundred men, hence the name "centurion." Cornelius's position was one of significant prestige and influence. He was also a "devout man and one who feared God" (10:2). As a result, he was a generous contributor to the synagogue. He was a Gentile, but he worshiped the God of Israel

Gentiles

The word translated "Gentiles" in Acts 11:1, 18 is the word *ethne*. Jesus used this same word in the Great Commission (Matthew 28:19–20). There it is translated "nations." *Ethne* is the root word for *ethnic* or *ethnicity*. James, Jesus' half-brother, used this term in his ruling at the Jerusalem council (Acts 15:17), quoting from Amos 9:11–12. The use of this term makes it clear that God included every ethnic group and nation in his redemptive plan from the beginning. John used the word *ethne* to describe the fulfillment of God's redemptive work at the end of time: "After these things I looked, and behold, a great multitude which no one could count, from every *nation* and all tribes and peoples and tongues, standing before the throne and before the Lamb, clothed in white robes . . ." (Revelation 7:9, italics added for emphasis).

even though he had not become a Jew ritually and officially. Most importantly, Cornelius was a man of prayer who "prayed to God continually" (10:2). When he was praying in the afternoon, at the ninth hour, or 3:00 P.M., an angel spoke to him and instructed him to send for Simon Peter, who was in Joppa (10:3–6). If Cornelius had not prayed he would not have received this instruction, and he would not have sent for Peter to tell him about Jesus.

> *Every believer needs to look within to discover the barriers that can prevent him or her from reaching all people with the gospel.*

In the New Testament, prayer was essential to crossing the barriers that would have prevented the gospel from reaching to the ends of the earth. This sort of prayer was very different from the prayers we often pray. Most of our prayers focus on our personal concerns for health, safety, and prosperity. For the first-century believers, prayer was the means by which God spoke to them. It is okay, of course, to pray for our daily needs and especially to give thanks to God for these things. But it is most important that we pray for God's kingdom to come on earth as it is in heaven (Matthew 6:10). When Paul was in prison, he asked for other believers to pray for him, not that he might be released, but that "God will open to us a door for the word. . . " (Colossians 4:3).

When my wife and I visited Seoul, Korea, a few years ago, we got up early one morning and went to church at 6:00 A.M. for prayer meeting. When we walked in, we found more than a thousand Korean Christians quietly and reverently praying, some alone, some in small groups of family and friends. Most often their prayers were whispered. We were deeply moved by this powerful gathering for prayer.

The first Protestant church was established in Korea in 1884. By 1984 more than 30,000 churches had been established. By 2000 this number grew to more than 60,000. South Korea is now the second largest mission-sending country in the world, with more than 10,000 missionaries serving throughout the world.[1] Many observers believe that the Korean Christians' devotion to prayer is the key to this remarkable growth.

Our Failure to See God's Vision Creates a Barrier to Doing All God Wants Us to Do

The central factor in this story is the vision God gave to Peter (Acts 10:9–16; 11:4–10). While Peter was praying on the housetop in Joppa, three times he saw a great sheet let down from heaven containing all manner of wildlife. In this vision, he received the command (10:13), "Get up, Peter, kill and eat!" At first, this vision didn't make any sense to Peter.

It was up to Peter to "connect the dots" in order to understand the meaning of this vision. When he received word that messengers had arrived from Cornelius asking him to come with them to Caesarea, he immediately made the connection. Without the vision, Peter might have dismissed the invitation, and the future of Christian missions might have been altered for all time.

Unless we consciously work at it, we will not be able to overcome the barriers of prejudice that keep us from seeing other people as individuals.

When we launched WorldconneX in 2004, we adopted the following purpose statement: "We connect God's people for God's vision."[2] We started by asking, *What is God's vision for you? What is God's vision for your church?* We soon discovered this presented a problem for most Christians and most churches. Most did not know what God's vision was for them.

I found many churches had adopted vision statements, but they still did not know what God's vision was for them. Finding God's vision for our church and our lives is very different from developing our own vision for God. God's vision originates from outside us and carries us in directions we might never have imagined.

Paul's experience on the second missionary journey is highly instructive here. Paul and his companions sought to go into Asia and Bithynia but were prevented by the Holy Spirit. Only after Paul came to Troas did he receive a vision in the night, a man of Macedonia asking him to come and help (16:6–10).

If we will prayerfully seek God's vision, laying aside our traditions and preconceived ideas to follow him obediently, God will use us to change the world.

God has a specific vision for each believer and each church that differs from God's vision for others. This was the same lesson Jesus taught Peter in John 21:15–23. There, when Peter asked Jesus what was going to happen to a fellow disciple, Jesus replied (John 21:21), ". . . What is that to you? You follow Me!"

We must be aware, too, that God gives us his vision for the next step of our journey with him. No one ever knows the full journey—where we will go or what we will do or how long we will live. But God guides us by sharpening our perception of his vision at strategic moments, turning points on the journey of faith and service.

So how do you find God's vision for your life and for your church? You must

(1) want God's vision more than you want your own
(2) commit yourself to prayer
(3) study the Scriptures
(4) discover how God made you and your church unique
(5) listen to what God is doing in the world
(6) listen to fellow believers
(7) be obedient in the things you know to do
(8) listen to your heart

Our Plans Can Become Barriers to Doing All God Wants Us to Do

The vision on the housetop came as an interruption to Peter. We have no idea what his plans were for the next day. Whatever they were, though, he laid them aside in order to obey the call of God (Acts 11:11–12). Often our plans become a barrier to reaching others. We are too busy to be interrupted.

> God's vision originates from outside us and carries us in directions we might never have imagined.

Much of what we know about Jesus came by what he said and did in interruptions: the woman at the well (John 4); the paralytic (Mark 2:1–12); the Gerasene demoniac (Mark 5:1–20); the woman with a hemorrhage of blood (Mark 5:25–34); blind Bartimaeus (Luke 18:35–43); and many others.

Our Lack of Obedience Creates Barriers to Doing All God Wants Us to Do

As soon as Peter understood the vision, he obeyed (Acts 10:19–23; 11:12). We often replace obedience with knowledge. This approach can create within us a false pride in our knowledge, including about the Bible. Many of the religious leaders of Jesus' day did not believe in him because they knew so much about the Bible that they were not teachable. Therefore, they were unwilling to obey him.

Jesus consistently focused on the importance of obedience. He concluded the Sermon on the Mount by saying, "Everyone who hears these words of Mine and *acts* on them, may be compared to a wise man who built his house on the rock" (Matthew 7:24, italics added for emphasis). At the Last Supper, Jesus said, "If you know these things, you are blessed if you *do* them" (John 13:17, italics added for emphasis).

Implications and Actions

Every believer needs to look within to discover the barriers that can prevent him or her from reaching all people with the gospel. If we will prayerfully seek God's vision, laying aside our traditions and preconceived ideas to follow him obediently, God will use us to change the world.

QUESTIONS

1. What traditions does your church have that keep your church from reaching people with the gospel?

2. How would you describe God's vision for your life?

3. How would you describe God's vision for your church?

4. Where have you observed prejudice most recently?

NOTES

1. Patrick Johnstone and Jason Mandryk, *Operation World* (Waynesboro, GA: Paternoster Publishing, 2001), 388.
2. See www.worldconnex.org.

6-3-07

Focal Text

Acts 11:19–26

Background

Acts 11:19–26

Main Idea

Missional churches seek ways to reach out to everyone.

Question to Explore

If the name "Christian" were not being used today, what would people in your church be called?

Study Aim

To identify ways in which our church could be encouraged to reach out to people more effectively

Study and Action Emphases

- Affirm the Bible as our authoritative guide for life and ministry
- Share the gospel with all people
- Develop a growing, vibrant faith
- Include all God's family in decision-making and service
- Value all people as created in the image of God
- Obey and serve Jesus by meeting physical, spiritual, and emotional needs
- Equip people for servant leadership

LESSON EIGHT

Reaching Out to Everyone

Quick Read

Antioch was the city where disciples were first called Christians. The story of Antioch helps us understand how churches can effectively reach people with the gospel everywhere.

I asked a veteran pastor how he communicated the gospel. Stuart Briscoe, pastor of Elmbrook Church in Brookfield, Wisconsin, for thirty years, had led this church to grow from less than two hundred to more than five thousand in attendance.

He said that when he first came to Elmbrook, he learned that if he asked people whether they were Christians, they would almost always say *yes*. But if he asked them whether they were disciples, they almost always said *no*. He then explained to them what it meant to be a disciple and how one became a disciple through faith in Jesus Christ.

Those who carried the gospel to Antioch had been scattered from Jerusalem by the persecution described in Acts 8:1, 4. We would call these people *laity*. Antioch was the capital of Syria, about 300 miles north of Jerusalem. It is not to be confused with Antioch of Pisidia (located in central Turkey), where Paul and Barnabas started a church later, on the first missionary journey (Acts 13:14). Syrian Antioch was a melting pot of the East and the West, a seaport crossroads with poor morals. Known as the *Queen of the East*, Antioch was the third largest city in the Roman Empire. Nicolas, one of the seven selected along with Stephen and Philip to serve the Jerusalem church in its ministry to widows, may have been the key contact (6:1–7). He was a native of Antioch. Nicolas was clearly a Gentile convert to Judaism since he is referred to as a "proselyte."

Acts 11:19–26

19So then those who were scattered because of the persecution that occurred in connection with Stephen made their way to Phoenicia and Cyprus and Antioch, speaking the word to no one except to Jews alone. 20But there were some of them, men of Cyprus and Cyrene, who came to Antioch and began speaking to the Greeks also, preaching the Lord Jesus. 21And the hand of the Lord was with them, and a large number who believed turned to the Lord. 22The news about them reached the ears of the church at Jerusalem, and they sent Barnabas off to Antioch. 23Then when he arrived and witnessed the grace of God, he rejoiced and began to encourage them all with resolute heart to remain true to the Lord; 24for he was a good man, and full of the Holy Spirit and of faith. And considerable numbers were brought to the Lord. 25And he left for Tarsus to look for Saul; 26and when he had found him, he brought him to Antioch. And for an entire year they met with the church and taught considerable numbers; and the disciples were first called Christians in Antioch.

To Reach People We Must Share
the Gospel with Everyone

When the disciples were scattered by the persecution, they made their way to Phoenicia, the narrow strip of land along the Mediterranean north of Galilee, and Cyprus, a large Mediterranean island about sixty miles off the coast of Phoenicia. They were "speaking the word" (11:19). But they did not speak the word to everyone. They shared their message only with those who were Jews.

But some of the believers who arrived in Antioch from Cyprus and Cyrene began witnessing to Greeks—Gentiles. The word translated "Greeks" (NASB, NIV) or "Grecians" (KJV), is *Ellenistas.* Our English word *Hellenistic* comes from this root. Unlike Nicolas, these Greeks were not converts to Judaism. If they had been, the church at Jerusalem would not have been concerned. These Gentiles responded to the gospel in large numbers.

Many of us are fairly comfortable with inviting someone to church. When we do, we usually employ a subconscious screening process. We consider whether they would be someone who would "fit in." Most often we invite people who look like us, talk like us, and have basically the same standard of living. We usually invite others who look like *church people.* Don't we?

When we decide to talk about Jesus to people who are different from us, though, everything changes. Many non-believers may be critical of churches and church people. But most people, even Muslims, have a high opinion of Jesus. They just don't know who Jesus really is or why Jesus came. Note that when these early believers spoke to the Greeks, they spoke about "the Lord Jesus" (11:20). They surely

We usually invite others who look like church *people. Don't we?*

told how Jesus died on the cross for our sins and how God raised Jesus from the dead. When they started talking about Jesus to non-Jews, they found a ready response.

I was going through a buffet line in a restaurant in Rochester, Minnesota. Stephanie, a young woman in her thirties, was behind me. I had been impressed with Stephanie's ability to reach out to others. She and her husband had established an outreach to the hockey players in Minnesota and were leading young men to Christ who had never attended church.

A young man was carving ham, turkey, and roast at the end of the buffet line. He had tattoos scrawled up both arms, as well as rings in each ear and in his nose. Without making eye contact, I asked for a couple of slices of ham and watched him carve the meat. Privately I was wondering how in the world he got this job and who would have hired him. Stephanie, though, asked him about the significance of his tattoos and the rings. He became animated and started to explain. Within minutes he was listening intently as Stephanie shared the gospel.

To Reach People We Must Live Transformed Lives

When Barnabas arrived and discovered what God was doing in Antioch, he immediately focused on the importance of spiritual health, encouraging them "with resolute heart to remain true to the Lord" (11:23). The remarkable growth at Antioch and the launch of the missions movement from this city (13:1–3) would not have occurred if the effort had not been built on healthy spiritual foundations.

If we would reach all people with the gospel in our generation, we must learn again what it means to be a disciple. The term *Christian* occurs only three times in the Bible, here in our focal text (see 11:26), in Acts 26:28, and also in 1 Peter 4:16. Jesus never used the term. Often those who believed were called followers of "the Way" (Acts 9:2; 19:9, 23; 24:14, 22; see also 22:4, "this Way"). The word *disciple* occurs numerous times in the New Testament. *Disciple* was the term Jesus used most often for those who followed him. The word *Christian* was first used at Antioch, coined not by the believers, but by non-believers. They created the term to indicate that those of "the Way" were *little Christs*. Apparently the believers spoke so much about Christ and followed Christ's teachings so clearly that the term *Christian* stuck.

Apparently the believers spoke so much about Christ and followed Christ's teachings so clearly that the term Christian stuck.

In our day the name *Christian* has come to mean many things. For some it means living a good moral life and being a good citizen. For some the term *Christian* includes the entire Western culture. Some consider themselves Christians because they were baptized as infants or simply because they are American and don't know what else they might be.

The influence of those who carried the message to Antioch was closely tied to their understanding that they were disciples. God had radically transformed their lives. Foremost of all, Jesus was Lord. This reality is why they were referred to as followers of "the Way." Without transformed lives, their message would have had little impact in Antioch.

One of the reasons churches do not reach people effectively in the United States is because non-Christians do not see transformed lives among church members. In the worst cases, churches suffer from ethical and moral failure among their leaders and their members. In others the lifestyle of those who claim to be Christians is so lukewarm that no appreciable difference between "Christians" and non-Christians is evident. The church and the culture have become identical.

> *Within minutes he was listening intently as Stephanie shared the gospel.*

To Reach People We Must Look For the Harvest

Our first thought may be that the apostles in Jerusalem sent Barnabas to Antioch in order to prevent heretical teaching, especially since Greeks were becoming believers. Maybe that's what indeed motivated them to send Barnabas. But perhaps there was another motive in their decision. Perhaps the apostles had learned from Jesus the strategic importance of looking for the harvest.

The harvest was one of Jesus' favorite metaphors (see, for example, Matthew 9:37–38; Luke 10:2; John 4:35). Jesus said, "Do you not say,

"Christians"

The believers were "first called Christians at Antioch" (Acts 11:26). The word translated "Christians" is *Christianous*, derived from the Greek word for *Christ*. Non-believers coined the term. In all his writing, Paul never used the term *Christian*. Peter was the only apostle to use the term. He used it once, in 1 Peter 4:16, a reference to being persecuted as a "Christian," a term used by the persecutors. In the next two centuries Roman emperors martyred many believers, referring to them as "Christians." But it is doubtful the believers used the term of themselves in the beginning. They identified themselves with secret symbols to avoid persecution as Christians. They identified themselves with the sign of the "fish" (*ixthus*) as an acronym for their faith—*Iesus Xristus THeou Uios Soterios* (transliteration of Greek words for *Jesus Christ God's Son Savior*).

'There are yet four months, and then comes the harvest'? Behold, I say to you, lift up your eyes, and look on the fields, that they are white for harvest" (John 4:35). He described his Father as "the Lord of the harvest" and instructed his disciples to pray that God would send workers into the harvest (Luke 10:2). In Luke 10 Jesus taught the disciples how to look for the harvest and how to engage in it.

In a sense, God is a *seasonal* God. Both the creation and Scripture reflect the importance of seasons, a time for planting and a time for harvest. Spiritual seasons of harvest occur among people groups, nations, and regions. In our time we are witnessing a season of harvest in Latin America, Africa, and Asia.[1] But harvest seasons do not last forever. Antioch, the birthplace of missions, is now predominantly Muslim. Jesus said, "We must work the works of Him who sent Me as long as it is day; night is coming when no one can work" (John 9:4).

In our day the name Christian has come to mean many things.

To Reach People We Must Encourage the Harvest

When the apostles chose Barnabas to visit Antioch, they chose the best encourager they could find. His birth name was Joseph. He was a Levite from Cyprus. But the name he earned by his character and behavior was "Barnabas," which meant "Son of Encouragement" (Acts 4:36). When Barnabas arrived in Antioch and discovered the evidence of God's grace among the believers, "he rejoiced and began to encourage them all. . . " (11:23). Sometimes the greatest gift you can give to the work of God is the gift of encouragement.

One of the reasons churches do not reach people effectively . . . is because non-Christians do not see transformed lives among church members.

When I first visited Guatemala in 2003 I found the leaders of the Guatemala Baptist Convention discouraged and dispirited. The International Mission Board had stopped working with them in 2000. In 2004 in a conference involving twenty leaders from across Guatemala, we encouraged them to discover God's vision. Others came alongside to encourage them, including Buckner Orphan Care, Baylor Health Care, Baptist University of the Americas, and Park Cities Baptist Church of Dallas. We returned in January 2006 to discover amazing results. Churches were growing, people were being reached, new churches were being started, and new ministries were springing up among Guatemala Baptists.

To Reach People We Must Connect Others to the Harvest

When Barnabas discovered what God was doing in Antioch, he thought of Saul of Tarsus. Barnabas had befriended Saul in Jerusalem some time earlier, when no one else wanted anything to do with him (see lesson 6 on Acts 9:10–28). We don't know how much time elapsed between Saul's conversion and Barnabas's invitation to join him at Antioch. By Paul's own account, three years passed before going to Jerusalem to visit the church leaders (Galatians 1:13–24). But Barnabas had kept up with him. Barnabas knew he could find Saul at his home in Tarsus (Acts 9:30; 11:25).

Tarsus was located northwest of Antioch in the province of Cilicia. By boat, it was only about fifty miles away. By land, it was approximately a hundred miles, traveling north on the highway from Antioch and joining the east-west trade route that connected Tarsus and the Euphrates.

How can you become effective in the work of God's kingdom?

Barnabas may have had several reasons for connecting Saul of Tarsus to the rapidly growing church in Antioch. Consider these: (1) Saul's Judaism was unquestioned (see Gal. 1:13–14; Philippians 3:4–6); (2) Saul was fluent in Greek, the common language of the Mediterranean world; (3) Saul was a scholar in the Scriptures, having studied under the great teacher Gamaliel (Acts 22:3); (4) God had revealed to Ananias that Saul was to be his instrument to the Gentiles (9:15).

How to Apply This Lesson

- List terms you could use to identify your faith other than the term *Christian.*
- If you have been on a mission trip outside the United States, review your experience and what you learned.
- If you have not been on a mission trip, visit with someone who has. Ask this person to describe the experience and what he or she learned.
- Find a new believer and offer encouragement.

Barnabas became convinced that connecting Saul of Tarsus to the young church at Antioch would be good both for Antioch and for Saul. So, rather than returning to Jerusalem, Barnabas set off to Tarsus to find his friend. Without this connection, Saul of Tarsus might never have been known as Paul the Apostle; the story of Acts might have never been written; and we might not have the letters of Paul. What an amazing difference the right connection at the right time can make.

To Reach People We Must Get Involved in the Harvest

Barnabas got involved in God's harvest at Antioch. For more than a year Barnabas and Saul taught Bible studies and became intimately involved in the life of the church at Antioch (11:26). This would set the stage for God's call to the church to set Barnabas and Saul apart as the first commissioned missionaries (13:1–3).

When we get involved where we are, doing what we can, sharing the message of Jesus with all people, God will open new doors of opportunity.

How can you become effective in the work of God's kingdom? Begin by getting involved where you are and doing what you can. In every city and many small towns you will find clusters of different people groups. Get involved. Start teaching a Bible study. If you travel internationally with your business, look for missions connections. When we get involved where we are, doing what we can, sharing the message of Jesus with all people, God will open new doors of opportunity. After all, God is the Lord of the harvest.

QUESTIONS

1. What kind of people do you feel comfortable inviting to your church?

2. If people who are different from you came to your church, would they fit in? Where? How?

3. When was the last time you talked with someone outside your church about Jesus?

4. What does being a disciple mean?

5. Whom do you know who needs to be connected to what God is doing in your church?

6. How are new believers nurtured and encouraged in your church?

NOTES

1. See Philip Jenkins, *The Next Christendom: The Coming of Global Christianity* (New York: Oxford University Press, 2002), 1–3.

On Mission to the World

Unit three follows Paul and his fellow missionaries as they extended the gospel beyond Jerusalem, Judea, and Samaria and, indeed, beyond simply Jews in these places. They shared the gospel with all people as they moved into all the world that they knew. The lessons are from the *witness to all the world* portion of Acts, which is Act 13:1—28:31.[1] The specific passages to be studied call us to engage in actions of ministry and witness to all people, although such actions may involve risk.

UNIT THREE. ON MISSION TO THE WORLD (ACTS 13:1—28:31)

Lesson 9	Risking to Follow God's Leadership	Acts 13:1–6a, 13–16, 42–52; 14:19–22
Lesson 10	Getting Refocused on Jesus	Acts 15:1–22a
Lesson 11	Inviting All Kinds of People to Christ	Acts 16:13–15, 25–34
Lesson 12	Sharing the Gospel with Skeptics	Acts 17:10–11, 16–34
Lesson 13	Ministering Inside, Reaching Outside	Acts 19:8–10; 20:18–35

NOTES

1. Unless otherwise indicated, all Scripture quotations in this unit introduction and lessons 9–13 are from the New International Version.

Focal Text

Acts 13:1–6a, 13–16,
42–52; 14:19–22

Background

Acts 13—14

Main Idea

Following God may
require taking what
appear to be risks.

Question to Explore

When's the last time
you or your church took
what appeared to be a
risk in order to follow
God's leadership?

Study Aim

To identify implications for me and my
church from how the early Christians
took what appeared to be risks in
order to follow God's leadership

Study and Action Emphases

- Affirm the Bible as our authoritative guide for
  life and ministry
- Share the gospel with all people
- Develop a growing, vibrant faith
- Include all God's family in decision-making
  and service
- Value all people as created in the image of
  God
- Obey and serve Jesus by meeting physical,
  spiritual, and emotional needs
- Equip people for servant leadership

LESSON NINE

Risking to Follow God's Leadership

Quick Read

Paul and Barnabas were willing to risk
discomfort, disapproval, and even death for the
sake of the gospel message entrusted to them
through their faith in Jesus Christ. Even the
church at Antioch had taken a risk in sending
them.

Even with all that has gone on so far in the Book of Acts, the Scripture for this lesson tells of a significant turning point in the life of the early church. This turning point required taking risks. Could taking what appear to be risks be a requirement for your church's truly becoming a missional church?

Let's remind ourselves of what had happened in the Book of Acts prior to this lesson. The Christians in the first church in Jerusalem had devoted themselves with a passion to the basic disciplines that lead to spiritual growth (Acts 2:42). As a result, God did great signs and wonders in their midst, and the church in Jerusalem experienced tremendous growth. When they came together to pray, God shook the place where they were. But they did only part of what the Risen Christ told them to do. In Acts 1:8, Jesus told the disciples to go to Jerusalem and to wait for the Holy Spirit, and when the Holy Spirit came upon them, Jesus promised, they would receive power. That part they had done. But they did not then do the other thing Jesus said. They did not go out as his witnesses, beyond Jerusalem, to "Judea and Samaria, and to the ends of the earth." They just stayed in Jerusalem. So Acts 8:1 states: "On that day a great persecution broke out against the church at Jerusalem, and all except the apostles were scattered throughout Judea and Samaria." Then, verse 4 adds: "Those who had been scattered preached the word wherever they went."

Why did that persecution come to the church? I cannot read the mind of God, and neither can I discern God's motivation in everything he does. But I believe it is a plausible scenario to suppose that when these first Christians refused to do voluntarily what Jesus told them to do, God allowed this persecution to come to the church to force the disciples to do what otherwise they would not do—move out of Jerusalem with the gospel and take it to the world.

But even then, this was merely an incidental implementation of the Acts 1:8 mandate, *until* a group of Christians in the church at Antioch finally got it! At Antioch, for the first time, the church intentionally implemented a strategy to carry out fully the Acts 1:8 mandate. This decision by the church at Antioch to move from accidental evangelism to strategic missions became the turning point in the history of the church. Let's see how it happened.

Acts 13:1–6a, 13–16, 42–52

1In the church at Antioch there were prophets and teachers: Barnabas, Simeon called Niger, Lucius of Cyrene, Manaen (who had been brought up with Herod the tetrarch) and Saul. **2**While they were worshiping the Lord and fasting, the Holy Spirit said, "Set apart for me Barnabas and Saul for the work to which I have called them." **3**So after they had fasted and prayed, they placed their hands on them and sent them off.

4The two of them, sent on their way by the Holy Spirit, went down to Seleucia and sailed from there to Cyprus. **5**When they arrived at Salamis, they proclaimed the word of God in the Jewish synagogues. John was with them as their helper.

6They traveled through the whole island until they came to Paphos.

. . . .

13From Paphos, Paul and his companions sailed to Perga in Pamphylia, where John left them to return to Jerusalem. **14**From Perga they went on to Pisidian Antioch. On the Sabbath they entered the synagogue and sat down. **15**After the reading from the Law and the Prophets, the synagogue rulers sent word to them, saying, "Brothers, if you have a message of encouragement for the people, please speak."

16Standing up, Paul motioned with his hand and said: "Men of Israel and you Gentiles who worship God, listen to me!"

. . . .

42As Paul and Barnabas were leaving the synagogue, the people invited them to speak further about these things on the next Sabbath. **43**When the congregation was dismissed, many of the Jews and devout converts to Judaism followed Paul and Barnabas, who talked with them and urged them to continue in the grace of God.

44On the next Sabbath almost the whole city gathered to hear the word of the Lord. **45**When the Jews saw the crowds, they were filled with jealousy and talked abusively against what Paul was saying.

46Then Paul and Barnabas answered them boldly: "We had to speak the word of God to you first. Since you reject it and do not consider yourselves worthy of eternal life, we now turn to the Gentiles. **47**For this is what the Lord has commanded us:

"'I have made you a light for the Gentiles,
that you may bring salvation to the ends of the earth.'"

48When the Gentiles heard this, they were glad and honored the word of the Lord; and all who were appointed for eternal life believed.

⁴⁹The word of the Lord spread through the whole region. ⁵⁰But the Jews incited the God-fearing women of high standing and the leading men of the city. They stirred up persecution against Paul and Barnabas, and expelled them from their region. ⁵¹So they shook the dust from their feet in protest against them and went to Iconium. ⁵²And the disciples were filled with joy and with the Holy Spirit.

Acts 14:19–22

¹⁹Then some Jews came from Antioch and Iconium and won the crowd over. They stoned Paul and dragged him outside the city, thinking he was dead. ²⁰But after the disciples had gathered around him, he got up and went back into the city. The next day he and Barnabas left for Derbe.

²¹They preached the good news in that city and won a large number of disciples. Then they returned to Lystra, Iconium and Antioch, ²²strengthening the disciples and encouraging them to remain true to the faith. "We must go through many hardships to enter the kingdom of God," they said.

Set Apart and Sent Out (13:1–6a)

The ancient city of Antioch was located in Syria, the territory just north of Galilee. Some of those scattered by the persecution of the church in Jerusalem had come to the city of Antioch with the gospel, and a "great number of people believed and turned to the Lord" (11:21). Since that "great number" included both Jews and Gentiles, the Antioch church took on a decidedly different look from that of the Christian congregation in Jerusalem. Jews and Gentiles were brought together by a common allegiance to Jesus Christ.

This decision by the church at Antioch to move from accidental evangelism to strategic missions became the turning point in the history of the church.

The church leaders in Jerusalem bristled at the picture of Jews and Gentiles sharing common fellowship around the table. So they sent Barnabas to investigate. Barnabas, in contrast, was elated with what he saw (11:23). So he brought Saul to Antioch. There, for a year, Barnabas and Saul taught the Christians at Antioch what it meant to be the church (11:26). The next word we hear about the church at Antioch is the picture given in our text, where the church leaders laid hands on Barnabas and Saul and intentionally sent them out as a part of a strategic plan to take the gospel to Gentiles as well as Jews.

As the text opens, the spotlight falls on five individuals who are called "prophets and teachers" (13:1). "Prophets" spoke forth the word of God. "Teachers" instructed the believers in the basics of the Christian life. Apparently, the five people listed carried out both responsibilities, for we can find no discernible distinction between roles and people in the text.

Saul and Barnabas both came from outside Antioch, and we will come to know them well as the story unfolds. But what of the other three? Luke identifies Simeon by his complexion, Lucius by his locale, and Manaen by his connection with Herod Antipas. Apart from this we know nothing more about them.

Of these five leaders, two were set aside to go out as missionaries (13:2). Notice that the church did not select these two. Instead, God's Spirit selected them. Being an Acts 1:8 church, a missional church, is not about getting God involved in our strategy. It is about us getting involved in God's strategy. God is the One who gifts us, calls us, and empowers us. All the church does is release people to fulfill

> *God is the One who gifts us, calls us, and empowers us.*

God's call. How do we do that? We do that by creating an environment in which God's Spirit can work. By "worshiping" and "fasting," the church

The Word of God

When the expression "the word of God" is used in the Book of Acts (4:31; 6:2, 7; 8:14; 11:1; 12:24; 13:7; 17:13; 18:11), in every instance it serves as a synonym for *the gospel.* Luke earlier described the preaching of Jesus as the "word of God" (Luke 5:1). In the parable of the sower, Jesus identified the "word of God" as the seed that is planted in the good soil that springs forth into eternal life (Luke 8:11).

In Luke and Acts, the term "the word of God" is not used in reference to a person (Jesus) or a book (the Scripture). Instead, Luke speaks of "the word of God" as the message from God that was proclaimed first by Jesus and then by the early church. Therefore, Luke talks about "the word of God" as being spoken (Acts 4:31), celebrates the spread of "the word of God" (6:7), and speaks of "the word of God" as being accepted (8:14). In Luke and Acts, the "word of God" is the message of the gospel shared by the early church.

at Antioch created that proper environment, and the Holy Spirit selected Barnabas and Saul.

Note the willingness of the church at Antioch to give up two of its best to do Christian work elsewhere. They might have considered doing so to be a risk, but they did it anyway.

Before the church sent Barnabas and Saul out, they did two things (13:3). First, they "fasted and prayed" (13:3). By these spiritual exercises, the Christians at Antioch acknowledged their total dependence on God. Fasting was often a sign of repentance, reflecting a desire to be reconnected to God. On this occasion, fasting was a sign of commitment, creating an attitude of prayer. Second, the church leaders "placed their hands on them" (13:3).

Note the willingness of the church at Antioch to give up two of its best to do Christian work elsewhere.

On three other occasions in the New Testament, as here in our text, the laying on of hands acknowledged the presence of spiritual gifts or a particular assignment to some individual (Acts 6:6; 1 Timothy 4:14; 2 Timothy 1:6). The act of laying on hands does not bestow these gifts or confer this assignment. That is the work of the Holy Spirit. Instead, laying on hands acknowledges what the Holy Spirit has already done.

In his brief summary of the opening days of this mission venture, Luke provides four insights (13:4–6a). First, he reminds us that this mission venture was not a human expedition but rather an endeavor empowered by the Holy Spirit. Second, he identifies the key stops on the itinerary: Seleucia, the seaport for Antioch, some sixteen miles from Antioch; Cyprus, an island directly off the coast of Syria, which was Barnabas's homeland; Salamis, a seaport village on the east coast of Cyprus; and Paphos, a town in the western part of Cyprus. Third, Luke further identifies the mission strategy Paul would follow throughout his life of witness for Christ. Saul and Barnabas went first to the synagogue to share the gospel. Why? The Jews who gathered to worship in each community that had a synagogue would understand more clearly Jesus' name and mission as the Messiah, for he was the fulfillment of the Jewish hope that someday God would send his Messiah to inaugurate his kingdom on earth. Finally, Luke mentions a "helper" who accompanied Barnabas and Saul, a young man named John. In Acts 15:37, Luke will identify this young helper as John Mark.

Encouraging support and outspoken criticism both appear as we carry out the work of the church.

Antioch: A Missional Church

To demonstrate in our churches today the missional principles reflected in the church at Antioch, we must

- Be intentional and not accidental in our mission strategy
- Create an environment in which the mission mandate is clearly understood
- Follow the Holy Spirit's leadership by releasing those who give evidence of having been called
- Send out our very best people to do the work of missions
- Be available to do the work of missions ourselves

Challenged and Strengthened (13:13–16, 42–52)

As the missionary party moved into Pamphylia, a small Roman province in southern Asia Minor, bordering the Mediterranean coast, young John Mark returned home, a move Saul interpreted as a lack of commitment (Acts 13:13; 15:38). Something else happened at this time. Saul begins to be referred to as Paul, and he became the leader of the group. The earlier references to "Barnabas and Saul" (13:2, 7) are now replaced by a reference to "Paul and his companions" (13:13).

We do not know what Paul and Barnabas did on this early leg of their missionary journey. Only when the party arrived in another city named Antioch, this one located in the Roman province of Pisidia, does Luke detail the missionaries' activity. Again, Paul and Barnabas went first to the synagogue. There they were invited to speak (13:15). Paul preached a message in which he described Jesus' life, death, and resurrection as the fulfillment of God's promise to Israel (13:16–41).

Paul's message evoked a positive response that provided an opportunity for dialogue with the members of the congregation and led to an invitation to return the following Sabbath to speak again (13:42). On the next Sabbath, though, the opposition of the Jewish leaders overwhelmed the eager anticipation among many in "the crowds" to hear these guests.

A closed door redirected Paul to another open door.

Consequently, Paul left the synagogue (13:46). However, this opposition by the Jewish leaders and the loss of opportunity to speak in the synagogue did not destroy the Christian mission to Antioch but simply redirected it. With the door closed to the Jews, Paul and Barnabas shared the gospel message with the Gentiles (13:46). Paul interpreted this redirection of their mission as a fulfillment of Isaiah's prophecy that the message of salvation would be proclaimed to all the earth (13:47; see Isaiah 49:6). A closed door redirected Paul to another open door.

> *Paul faced his fear and then moved through it, driven by a passionate desire to please God and to share God's word with the world.*

Conflicting emotions intermingled as Paul and Barnabas completed their ministry in Antioch of Pisidia. On the one hand, Paul and Barnabas experienced the thrill of victory as the gospel was "spread through the whole region" (Acts 13:49). On the other hand, they were driven out of the region by a protest led by the most powerful people in the city (13:50). On the one hand, Paul and Barnabas experienced disappointment, causing them to shake the dust from their feet as they left the city. On the other hand, they were "filled with joy" (13:52).

How often we experience the same conflicting emotions in our service for the Lord today. Encouraging support and outspoken criticism both appear as we carry out the work of the church. Hurt and joy often coincide in the same experience. A sense of failure often dilutes a briefly held sense of accomplishment. Ministry is sometimes difficult. We can perhaps be encouraged by remembering that whenever we experience the difficulties of ministry today, we are simply moving along in the same stream as Paul and Barnabas. They faced these same conflicting responses and emotions in their ministry to the people of Antioch of Pisidia nearly 2,000 years ago.

Stymied but Not Stopped (14:19–22)

The conflict continued as Paul and Barnabas moved from Iconium, one of the chief cities in the southern part of the Roman province of Galatia, to Lystra, just to the south of the city of Iconium. Lystra was a Roman colony. At Lystra, the opposition to these Christian missionaries erupted into an explosion of anger. The crowd dragged Paul outside the city and stoned him, leaving him for dead (14:19).

God, though, was not through with Paul yet. God preserved his life for further ministry. Luke does not say Paul was brought back from the dead. However, the amazing turnaround from being left for dead one moment and then in the next instant being back on his feet again suggests some kind of miraculous intervention. Perhaps even more amazing, Paul went back into the very city where he had been stoned. Paul would not be controlled by his fear, and neither would he be intimidated by bullies. Paul illustrated a truth many still demonstrate today: *Courage is not the absence of fear but the willingness to act in the midst of fear.* Paul faced his fear and then moved through it, driven by a passionate desire to please God and to share God's word with the world.

Paul gave additional evidence of his courage when he moved to Derbe, a city southeast of Lystra. In Derbe, the preaching of the gospel produced many converts (14:21). Did Paul originally plan to go to Derbe? Or did he go there simply to allow things to cool off in Lystra? We cannot be sure. If the latter was the case, then God again used a closed door (driven from Lystra) into an open door (a field ripe for harvest in Derbe).

Then Paul and Barnabas returned to the cities where he had been opposed, criticized, threatened, and even left for dead. Paul was not seeking sympathy from the Christians in these cities. Instead, he returned to these cities where he had established new churches. He did so for two specific reasons. First, he wanted to organize the kingdom work that had begun in response to the preaching of the gospel (14:23). Perhaps more importantly, Paul and Barnabas wanted to encourage these new believers with a call to faithfulness, a challenge given extra credibility because of the unswerving faithfulness Paul demonstrated in his own life. In other words, Paul did not ask the new converts to do anything he was not willing to do himself. Both with his life and with his lips, Paul reminded the Christians all along the way that the Christian life is not a life of ease or unending bliss. Rather, such a life may be one of continuous crises, and it calls for courageous faith.

Proponents of the *health-and-wealth* gospel imply that a person of faith will be blessed materially and circumstantially. They evidently have not read the Book of Acts. Both the demonstrations of and the remonstrations against the first-century Christians whose stories are told in the Book of Acts clearly reveal that the life of faith usually stirs up opposition and is often lived out in the crucible of suffering. That was Paul's experience. He promised the same to the converts of his first missionary journey. We should expect nothing different today.

QUESTIONS

1. As you evaluate the mission strategy of your church, do you think it is more *accidental* or more *intentional?*

2. What lessons can we learn from the example of the Antioch church concerning a more strategic approach to missions?

3. What is your church doing to call out people to serve God, including service as ministers and missionaries?

4. Can you think of an example of unusual courage displayed by someone in your church who was carrying out the work of God?

5. Do you think we are willing to risk as much for the faith today as Paul and Barnabas did in our text? If not, why not?

Focal Text

Acts 15:1–22a

Background

Acts 15:1–35

Main Idea

The church must continue to focus on Jesus, proclaiming that only faith in him is needed for salvation, with no other requirement.

Question to Explore

What else is needed for salvation other than faith in Jesus? Do we ever add anything?

Study Aim

To summarize the concerns of the Jerusalem council and reaffirm that salvation is by faith in Jesus alone, with nothing else added

Study and Action Emphases

- Affirm the Bible as our authoritative guide for life and ministry
- Share the gospel with all people
- Develop a growing, vibrant faith
- Include all God's family in decision-making and service
- Value all people as created in the image of God
- Obey and serve Jesus by meeting physical, spiritual, and emotional needs

LESSON TEN
Getting Refocused on Jesus

Quick Read

At the Jerusalem council, the first-century church affirmed that salvation comes through faith in Jesus Christ alone, with nothing else required.

Have you ever studied the business meeting minutes from the earlier history of your church? Humorous entries often stand alongside discussions of heated debate about serious issues. For example, while I was pastor of the First Baptist Church in Pensacola, Florida, I spent some time reviewing the church conference reports that went all the way back to that historic day in May 1847 when the church was organized.

In the conference on July 1, 1881, I found these two entries:

- First, Sister Susan Fleming acknowledged to the church that she was guilty of dancing. She declared that she wished to be forgiven by the church and promised not to be guilty of such conduct any more. On motion of a certain member of the church, Sister Susan was forgiven.
- At the same meeting a resolution was passed decreeing that any male member who missed two regular church conferences in a row, without a good excuse, would be declared out of order. I don't know exactly what happened to a person when he was "declared out of order," but it sounds serious!

These two issues in that one church conference don't seem that important to us today, but many church conferences have provided the setting in which the church debated important issues. The decisions reached were momentous for the history of that particular church. What is true today was also true of the first-century church. Different opinions about the nature of salvation threatened to split the young church. So leaders of all sides gathered in Jerusalem around A.D. 48 for a crucial church conference.

Acts 15:1–22a

[1]Some men came down from Judea to Antioch and were teaching the brothers: "Unless you are circumcised, according to the custom taught by Moses, you cannot be saved." [2]This brought Paul and Barnabas into sharp dispute and debate with them. So Paul and Barnabas were appointed, along with some other believers, to go up to Jerusalem to see the apostles and elders about this question. [3]The church sent them on their way, and as they traveled through Phoenicia and Samaria, they told how the Gentiles had been converted. This news made all the brothers very glad.

[4]When they came to Jerusalem, they were welcomed by the church and the apostles and elders, to whom they reported everything God had done through them.

[5]Then some of the believers who belonged to the party of the Pharisees stood up and said, "The Gentiles must be circumcised and required to obey the law of Moses."

[6]The apostles and elders met to consider this question. [7]After much discussion, Peter got up and addressed them: "Brothers, you know that some time ago God made a choice among you that the Gentiles might hear from my lips the message of the gospel and believe. [8]God, who knows the heart, showed that he accepted them by giving the Holy Spirit to them, just as he did to us. [9]He made no distinction between us and them, for he purified their hearts by faith. [10]Now then, why do you try to test God by putting on the necks of the disciples a yoke that neither we nor our fathers have been able to bear? [11]No! We believe it is through the grace of our Lord Jesus that we are saved, just as they are." ✳

[12]The whole assembly became silent as they listened to Barnabas and Paul telling about the miraculous signs and wonders God had done among the Gentiles through them. [13]When they finished, James spoke up: "Brothers, listen to me. [14]Simon has described to us how God at first showed his concern by taking from the Gentiles a people for himself. [15]The words of the prophets are in agreement with this, as it is written:

[16] "'After this I will return
and rebuild David's fallen tent.
Its ruins I will rebuild,
and I will restore it,
[17] that the remnant of men may seek the Lord,
and all the Gentiles who bear my name,
says the Lord, who does these things'
[18] that have been known for ages.

[19]"It is my judgment, therefore, that we should not make it difficult for the Gentiles who are turning to God. [20]Instead we should write to them, telling them to abstain from food polluted by idols, from sexual immorality, from the meat of strangled animals and from blood. [21]For Moses has been preached in every city from the earliest times and is read in the synagogues on every Sabbath."

[22]Then the apostles and elders, with the whole church, decided to choose some of their own men and send them to Antioch with Paul and Barnabas.

The Dissension (15:1–5)

Initially the church attracted only Jews who were committed to the Jewish law and who rested in the cradle of Jewish custom. But then something new happened. The Christian faith expanded beyond the boundaries of Jerusalem and beyond the ranks of the Jews.

On the Gaza road, for example, Philip shared the gospel with an Ethiopian eunuch who possibly was a Jew but in my view was a God-fearer (a Gentile who was attracted to the monotheism and moral teachings of Judaism). After he professed faith in Jesus, Philip baptized him (Acts 8:34–39; see lesson five).

Inspired by a vision from the Lord, Peter went to Caesarea and shared the gospel with Cornelius, a Gentile who is described as being "God-fearing" (10:2). When Cornelius and his family professed faith in Jesus, Peter baptized them. The Holy Spirit confirmed the genuineness of their conversion by coming upon them just as the Spirit had done for the initial Jewish believers at Pentecost (10:44–48).

We sometimes mistakenly long for the good old days of the church when everyone got along with everyone else.

Then, the Christians who were scattered by the Jerusalem persecution traveled to Antioch. They shared the gospel with the Gentiles there, and "a great number of people believed and turned to the Lord" (11:21). The blossoming church in Antioch caught the attention of the believers in Jerusalem, and so they sent Barnabas to investigate. Barnabas gave the church his stamp of approval (11:23). From the church in Antioch came the first strategic effort to fulfill the Acts 1:8 commission. We examined the results of that effort in last week's lesson. As a result of all these efforts, Jews and Gentiles (and even Samaritans, Acts 8:5) came together in a preview of the new unity of believers Paul would later describe in his Letter to the Ephesians (Ephesians 2:14–18).

Ironically, some of the Christian leaders in Jerusalem were not happy about this new development. Their concept of Christianity was cast in a definite Jewish tint. So dissension erupted in the first-century church over the nature of salvation.

On one side were those who believed the Christian faith had to blossom in a Jewish context. Those holding this view are identified in our text as "believers who belonged to the party of the Pharisees" (Acts 15:5). The expression of their position brackets this part of our text (15:1, 5). Who

The Pharisees

The Pharisees were one of the three prominent parties in Judaism during the time of Christ. (The other two were the Sadducees and the Essenes.) *Pharisees* literally means *the separated ones.* The word describes a group of Jewish leaders, established during the interbiblical period, who desired to separate themselves from the common Jews by an extraordinary attention to following the Jewish law. By the first century, the Pharisees had established a rigid discipline of life by which they believed a person could obtain a good standing with God.

The Pharisees inevitably clashed with Jesus. Jesus taught that a disciplined life was the *result* of a good standing with God, not the cause of it. The believers identified as being of "the party of the Pharisees" (Acts 15:5) were therefore Christians who emphasized an adherence to the law as a requirement for being a Christian. The Jerusalem conference decided against this position. Consequently, after the Jerusalem conference the terms "believer" and "party of the Pharisees" became incompatible terms.

---

were these people? Many commentators identify them with the delegation sent by James cited in Galatians 2:12, although we cannot be certain of that identification.

What we can be certain of is their position on salvation. They believed that faith in Jesus Christ was not sufficient to bring a person to salvation. They added two requirements. "Circumcision" was one requirement (Acts 15:1, 5). That is, a person had to identify with the Jewish religious rituals. Too, a person also had to follow the Jewish law (15:5). Such a radical reinterpretation struck at the heart of the gospel. The gospel offered salvation to "whoever believes" in Jesus (John 3:16) and whoever

Both sides needed to state their position so that the church could reach a decision everyone could live with.

"calls on the name of the Lord" (Romans 10:13). These legalists went to Antioch to articulate their position (Acts 15:1).

On the other side were those whose experience had shattered the limitations of the legalists. They welcomed into the church any person of any ethnic or religious group who would acknowledge Jesus as Lord (15:2–4). This was the position of the church at Antioch. The church once again appointed Paul and Barnabas, this time to go to Jerusalem as champions for the gospel.

Note that Paul and Barnabas did not argue from Old Testament precedent. They simply shared what they had experienced on their missionary journey through Asia Minor (15:4).

We sometimes mistakenly long for the *good old days* of the church when everyone got along with everyone else. Unfortunately, the church has never known such *good old days*. Even in the earliest period of the church's history, Christians held conflicting opinions that often created dissension among the members of the family of God.

We can learn a lesson from the Christians at Antioch. They were not willing to ignore the tension between them and their fellow Christians in Jerusalem. Neither were they willing to cave in with the hope of creating an artificial harmony. Instead, they acknowledged the problem. They then attempted to dissolve the problem by sending delegates to Jerusalem to participate in the conference. They did not allow fear of the Jerusalem Christians to deter them from their convictions. Instead, when Paul and Barnabas passed through "Phoenicia and Samaria," they openly shared the gospel with the local citizens and testified clearly how other non-Jews had been converted (15:3). A cordial welcome also greeted them when they arrived in Jerusalem (15:4). This cordial welcome did not signal complete concurrence with their position, however. Both sides needed to state their position so that the church could reach a decision everyone could live with.

Like Paul, we must all testify that it is only through Christ that we can accomplish all things (Philippians 4:13).

The Discussion (15:6–12)

We do not know how many attended this momentous conference. Luke suggests a rather large attendance with his references to "the whole assembly" in Acts 15:12 and "the whole church" in Acts 15:22.

Among the crowd Luke identified "the apostles and elders" (15:6). "Apostle" was used in both an official sense and in a more general sense in the New Testament. On some occasions, the term identified the Twelve selected by Jesus as his special companions (Matthew 10:2). Matthias, who replaced Judas, inherited that identity as well (Acts 1:26). But the term was also used in a general way to identify leaders of the first-century church like James (Gal. 1:19); Barnabas and Paul (Acts 14:14); Adronicus and Junias (Rom. 16:7); and Silas (1 Thess. 1:1; 2:6). *Apostle* in this general sense seems to be the case in our text.

"Elders" parallels "bishops" in other New Testament references (see Acts 20:17, 28; Titus 1:5, 7). They were appointed as leaders of individual churches (Acts 14:23). So these unidentified delegates at the Jerusalem conference were leaders of the various groups of believers who—along with Peter, James, Paul, and Barnabas—participated in a lengthy debate about the nature of salvation. James, the brother of Jesus, presided over the conference. The three keynote speakers were Peter, Paul, and Barnabas.

Peter did not argue about the issue. He simply told the story of his experience in Caesarea when he shared the gospel with Cornelius and his family (10:24; 15:7–11). But this was not really Peter's story. This was God's story. God was the One who sent him

Salvation through Christ is available to everyone who believes.

to the Gentile Cornelius (15:7). God was the One who confirmed the salvation of Cornelius and his family by giving his Holy Spirit (15:8). Too, God was the One who "purified their hearts by faith" (15:9). To claim that the conversion of Cornelius and his family was not genuine was to question the character of God.

Earlier Peter had expressed his feeling even more strongly in the description of his experience with Cornelius. As a lifelong Jew, Peter was himself startled by what happened at Cornelius's house. It broke his paradigm concerning salvation and made him uncomfortable. Nevertheless, he could not question the reality of Cornelius's salvation because God had confirmed it. Peter bluntly asked (11:17): "Who was I to think that I could oppose God?"

Then Paul and Barnabas took the floor. Like Peter, they did not argue

The First Lord's Supper

It was to be the eight-year-old's first Lord's Supper. The week before, he had made his profession of faith. When he heard that the church was having the Lord's Supper the next Sunday, he was excited. However, the next Sunday, as the elements were being passed, the person sitting next to the boy told him that he could not participate in the Lord's Supper because he had not yet been baptized and the Lord's Supper was only for baptized believers. If you were the boy's parent, how would you have responded?

the issue. They simply told the story of their experiences throughout Asia Minor where individuals with no Jewish background who did not follow the customs of Jewish law nevertheless experienced salvation through their faith in Jesus Christ (15:12). Luke gives few details about the content of the stories Paul and Barnabas shared with the conference. Although their stories were different from Peter's story, they essentially paralleled Peter's. Paul and Barnabas, like Peter, acknowledged that these stories were not about what they had done but about what God had done.

The requirement of salvation is Jesus alone—not Jesus plus baptism, not Jesus plus circumcision, not Jesus plus church membership, not Jesus plus anything.

We could learn from all three of these who testified at the first church conference. Too often our testimonies magnify how many great accomplishments we have made for God's kingdom, perhaps including how many people we have brought to the Lord. A little humility is in order. We do not bring anyone to the Lord. God does that himself. We do not accomplish anything on our own. Like Paul, we all must testify that it is only through Christ that we can accomplish all things (Philippians 4:13).

The Decision (15:13–22a)

By this point, the weight of testimony pointed so clearly in a single direction that James, who apparently moderated this church conference, summed up the appropriate decision. Notice that those who attended the conference did not vote on one or the other position. After the time of discussion, James simply articulated what was clearly God's decision, reflected through the multiple experiences of Peter and Barnabas and Paul.

James set his conclusion in the context of Scripture. Drawing together quotes from Amos 9:11–12; Jeremiah 12:15; and Isaiah 45:21, James concluded that what happened was nothing less than a fulfillment of what the prophets had foretold centuries earlier (Acts 15:16–18). The heart of the quote is drawn from Amos 9:12, where the prophet pointed to a time when "all the nations that bear my name" will be included among God's remnant.

Standing on this scriptural foundation, James articulated a position on the two issues before the Jerusalem conference. Concerning the nature of salvation, James was unequivocal. They should add nothing to what God had already affirmed (Acts 15:19). Salvation through Christ is available to everyone who believes.

Concerning the nature of fellowship between those who believe, the solution was not as simple. To facilitate fellowship between Jewish Christians and Gentile Christians, James suggested four basic guidelines (15:20–21). Three of these guidelines had to do with etiquette for table fellowship. One of them related to moral character. We must remember, however, that these guidelines had nothing to do with salvation. They were guidelines to facilitate fellowship between those who were already saved.

> *. . . We need to identify with, associate with, cooperate with, and fellowship with God's people.*

Once God's will became clear to those who attended the conference, they took specific steps to communicate that decision to the church in Antioch. They fashioned a letter to be delivered to the Antioch church. Too, they designated Judas and Silas to accompany Barnabas and Paul as they delivered the letter to the church.

Did this permanently solve the problem? No. The debate continued, but a stake had been nailed in the ground that would be the tethering rod for the evangelistic efforts of the first-century church. Any person could become a Christian through faith in Jesus Christ. Nothing more was required. That's still the case.

Implications and Actions

This Jerusalem conference played a pivotal role in the early development of the church, for several reasons. The Jerusalem conference was significant because of what it decided about the requirement of salvation. At that historic conference in Jerusalem, the church confirmed that Jesus alone can save. The requirement of salvation is Jesus alone—not Jesus plus baptism, not Jesus plus circumcision, not Jesus plus church membership, not Jesus plus anything.

In addition, the Jerusalem conference was significant because of what it revealed about the result of salvation. What happens to a Christian when he or she is saved? Behind the guidelines for fellowship suggested to the Gentiles (15:20) is the basic presupposition that when we become a Christian we become a part of God's family. Therefore we need to identify with, associate with, cooperate with, and fellowship with God's people.

QUESTIONS

1. Do you see evidence in the church today that some people still want to add a requirement to salvation in addition to faith in Jesus? If so, what is an example?

2. Why does that thinking persist in the church even today?

3. What can you do to affirm the decision reached by the Jerusalem conference concerning the requirement for salvation?

4. How does the pattern of dealing with conflict in your church compare to the pattern reflected in our text?

Focal Text
Acts 16:13–15, 25–34

Background
Acts 15:36—16:40

Main Idea
The message of Christ is good news for all kinds of people.

Question to Explore
To what extent does your church act on the recognition that the message of Christ is good news for all kinds of people?

Study Aim
To compare Lydia and the jailer and to identify ways for extending our church's ministry to all people

Study and Action Emphases

- Affirm the Bible as our authoritative guide for life and ministry
- Share the gospel with all people
- Develop a growing, vibrant faith
- Include all God's family in decision-making and service
- Value all people as created in the image of God
- Obey and serve Jesus by meeting physical, spiritual, and emotional needs
- Equip people for servant leadership

LESSON ELEVEN

Inviting All Kinds of People to Christ

Quick Read
Paul's experience at Philippi confirms that the power of the gospel draws all kinds of people to Jesus, regardless of previous experience or personal background.

I'll never forget the night. It was one of the most disappointing times in my ministry. Our church was considering expanding our facilities, and we called a Town Hall meeting to discuss the need and determine what we should do. We were out of space for our adult Bible study participants, and I was convinced that the time had come for us to build.

We labeled the area directly around our church as our Red Zone. Our research revealed that at least 350,000 people lived within the area we marked out as our Red Zone. That meant that 350,000 people lived within fifteen minutes drive time from our church. The area included many different ethnic groups and age demographics. Not more than forty percent of these people attended any church. They were a field ripe for the harvest, and I suggested to our congregation that we needed to provide larger facilities to prepare for the people we were going to reach in our Red Zone.

One of our members stood up during the discussion time and said, "I think this Red Zone the pastor has been talking about is a myth. I don't think there are that many people around us, and besides, these people in our neighborhood are not even our kind of people anyway." Somewhere along the line, I had failed to communicate effectively to the congregation that every person is "our kind of people."

The New Testament church worked through that issue in the Jerusalem conference (Acts 15), and they determined that everyone was "their kind of people." Armed with that reaffirmation, Paul and Silas headed out for another mission trip. Along the way, they came to the city of Philippi. While they were there, they introduced the gospel to a number of very different kinds of people. We'll look more closely at two of these people. But first let's set the context for the evangelistic efforts in Philippi.

Acts 16:13–15, 25–34

¹³On the Sabbath we went outside the city gate to the river, where we expected to find a place of prayer. We sat down and began to speak to the women who had gathered there. ¹⁴One of those listening was a woman named Lydia, a dealer in purple cloth from the city of Thyatira, who was a worshiper of God. The Lord opened her heart to respond to Paul's message. ¹⁵When she and the members of her household were baptized, she invited us to her home. "If you consider me a believer in the Lord," she said, "come and stay at my house." And she persuaded us.

²⁵About midnight Paul and Silas were praying and singing hymns to God, and the other prisoners were listening to them. ²⁶Suddenly there was such a violent earthquake that the foundations of the prison were shaken. At once all the prison doors flew open, and everybody's chains came loose. ²⁷The jailer woke up, and when he saw the prison doors open, he drew his sword and was about to kill himself because he thought the prisoners had escaped. ²⁸But Paul shouted, "Don't harm yourself! We are all here!"

²⁹The jailer called for lights, rushed in and fell trembling before Paul and Silas. ³⁰He then brought them out and asked, "Sirs, what must I do to be saved?"

³¹They replied, "Believe in the Lord Jesus, and you will be saved—you and your household." ³²Then they spoke the word of the Lord to him and to all the others in his house. ³³At that hour of the night the jailer took them and washed their wounds; then immediately he and all his family were baptized. ³⁴The jailer brought them into his house and set a meal before them; he was filled with joy because he had come to believe in God—he and his whole family.

Paul and Silas Go to Philippi (16:1–12)

As the second missionary journey began, a conflict arose between Paul and Barnabas concerning John Mark's suitability to come along on this second trip. As a result, Paul had to find a new partner. He chose Silas. The two of them headed west (Acts 15:36–41).

In one brief paragraph, Luke mentions the travels of the group through Phrygia, Galatia, and Mysia, coming eventually to the city of Troas on the eastern shore of the Aegean Sea (16:6–8). Study the map of that area and you will realize what a vast area this journey covered and what a long period of time these travels must have consumed.

This band of missionaries was not zooming along some superhighway or racing along in a fast-moving train. They traveled on foot for hundreds of miles. What were they doing during these days? Where all did they travel in these areas? Luke doesn't tell us. He finally slows down his narrative when Paul arrived at Troas. Here, Paul had a vision of a man calling him to come over to Macedonia. So Paul crossed the Aegean Sea and came to the province of Macedonia, to the city of Philippi.

Macedonia was located between the Balkan highlands and the peninsula we know as modern Greece. Thessalonica, Berea, and Philippi were cities in Macedonia. Strategically located and politically important, Philippi was a Roman colony, which meant that Philippi had the right of self-government and land ownership. As a colony, this city was in essence a little piece of Rome located in the province of Macedonia. Luke refers to Philippi as "the leading city" of that part of Macedonia (16:12). So Paul began his evangelistic effort there.

Luke tells the story of three individuals in Philippi who responded positively to the gospel: the businesswoman Lydia (16:14); the possessed slave girl (16:16); and the jailer (16:27). These three people were from different levels of society, they had different spiritual needs, and they looked at life from different perspectives. Yet, they were tied together by the common thread of a shared experience with the gospel of Jesus Christ. This is not an exhaustive list of those who came to know Jesus in Philippi but rather a sampling. A woman named Lydia who was searching for God satisfied her quest in Jesus Christ. A girl who was under the control of Satan found release in Jesus Christ. A man who was hardened by years of calloused living found transformation in Jesus Christ. Three distinct people from different backgrounds came to know Christ through Paul's efforts in Philippi. Luke describes two of these conversion experiences in our primary text for this lesson. The first one is the businesswoman named Lydia.

This man would certainly fit into the category that one of my church members identified as "not our kind of people."

Reaching a Businesswoman Who Prayed (16:13–15)

Normally Paul began his ministry in a city in the synagogue. There he would find Jews who could connect more readily with his message about Jesus as the Messiah and the fulfillment of God's promises to Israel. However, in Philippi, Paul went first to a group of women who met regularly for prayer by the river. Does this mean that Philippi did not have a large enough Jewish population to justify a synagogue? Some scholars interpret Paul's action in that way. Whenever ten Jewish men lived in a community, they would develop a synagogue. Apparently, Philippi had an extremely small Jewish population. Or was

" . . . These people . . . are not even our kind of people anyway."

124

Paul just so unfamiliar with the city of Philippi that he did not know where the synagogue was? Other scholars interpret Paul's action in this way. Luke does not explain Paul's motives, though. He simply says that the missionary team received information about a group of women who prayed outside the city gate, next to the river. When the missionary group went there, they found them just as they had expected.

Among the women in the prayer group was a woman named Lydia. She was a businesswoman, "a dealer in purple cloth" (16:14). Thyatira, her hometown, was known for producing dyes used to color cloth. We don't know why she now resided in Philippi. Evidently, though, she was a woman of wealth, because she had her own house and her own servants (16:15). Even more important, Lydia was "a worshiper of God" (16:14). Whether this means she was a God-fearer, a Gentile who had been drawn to the worship of Israel's God, or whether this means she was an actual proselyte to Judaism, is not clear. What is clear is that her heart was attuned to God. She was thus fertile soil for the seed of the gospel.

> *Then Grace took me to another neighbor and to another until finally seven women acknowledged their faith in Christ.*

Grace and her friends were like that (not her real name). She had brought her child to our church to participate in our after-school care. So I went by to see her late one afternoon. I talked to her about the church.

Believer

The common thread in the experience of both Lydia and the jailer is the concept of faith or belief. Lydia is spoken of as a "believer" (Acts 16:15). Too, about the jailer, Luke says that he "was filled with joy because he had come to believe in God" (16:34).

To *believe* is a central New Testament concept. What does it mean?

The word *believe* is used a number of different ways in the New Testament. When used to describe the Christian life, though, to *believe* means to enter into a relationship of trust with Jesus. Likewise, to be a *believer* does not mean to hold a certain set of convictions about Jesus or God but to be in a relationship with God through Jesus Christ. In several instances, God is the object of this belief (see Acts 16:34), but usually the New Testament writers speak of believing in Jesus (see 1 John 3:23). As "the way and the truth and the life" (John 14:6), Jesus is the object of our faith. To be in a relationship with Jesus is to be in a relationship with God.

Then I shared more specifically about what it means to be a Christian, and she invited Jesus into her heart. Before I left, she said, "I have a neighbor I want you to talk to." This neighbor also received Jesus. Then Grace took me to another neighbor and to another until finally seven women acknowledged their faith in Christ. They were all baptized together in a night of celebration at our church.

According to the New Testament, only one pathway leads to salvation, and that is the pathway of faith.

We see a similar pattern in our text. Luke tells us that "the Lord opened her heart to respond to Paul's message" (16:14). Into the fertile soil of Lydia's life the gospel seed was planted, and it sprang forth into eternal life. She invited Paul to share the message with "the members of her household," and they too acknowledged Jesus as their Savior (16:15). She wanted others to hear the message as well. So she invited Paul and Silas to make her home a meeting place for those who wanted to hear more about the gospel. Her house would eventually become the center of a growing Christian movement in Philippi (16:40).

Reaching a Jailer Who Was a Pagan (16:25–34)

Not everyone in Philippi approved of these traveling evangelists who had come to their city. When Paul converted a slave girl who had made her masters a great deal of money by telling fortunes, the spark of discontent ignited into a raging fire of malice. To settle the conflagration, the magistrates arrested Paul and Silas, beat them, and threw them into prison (16:16–24). In prison, Paul came in contact

"All of you out there, come on back in, for it was just for such as you that Jesus died."

with an unlikely candidate for the gospel. This man would certainly fit into the category that one of my church members identified as "not our kind of people." Yet, the gospel was for him as well, as the unfolding story reveals.

Don't miss the remarkable reaction to suffering demonstrated by Paul and Silas. They had been beaten. Then they were tossed into the Philippian jail. Then they were placed in a more secure place—"the inner cell"—and put in stocks (16:24). So what did they do? They sang hymns (16:25)! By their attitude and by the words of their hymns, Paul and Silas witnessed to the other prisoners, for Luke tells us that "the other prisoners were listening to them" (16:25).

How we respond to the difficult circumstances of our lives is a witness to others. What kind of witness do we give?

At that point, God intervened. An earthquake shook the foundations of the prison, opening all the doors of the prison and releasing all the prisoners. The earthquake also awakened the jailer. He panicked when he saw the doors open, thinking the prisoners had escaped. Before he could harm himself, Paul alerted him that all the prisoners were still in their cells. Awed by the divine intervention that he quickly connected with his newest prisoners, the jailer asked them (16:30), "What must I do to be saved?" Why did he ask that question? Perhaps he had heard the stories about this new message presented by these newcomers to Philippi. No doubt he knew of the reason for their arrest. Too, likely he had heard them singing in their cells. Also, the divine intervention gave credibility to everything he had heard about them. So he wanted to know how he could be saved from his life of emptiness and hopelessness.

> *So he wanted to know how he could be saved from his life of emptiness and hopelessness.*

Paul's response is the basic New Testament response to the question, *What must a person do to be saved?* Salvation does not come by good works. Salvation is not obtained by righteous living. Salvation cannot be earned by religious ritual. According to the New Testament, only one pathway leads to salvation, and that is the pathway of faith. Not only the jailer but his entire family chose to follow that pathway, and each experienced the salvation that comes through Jesus Christ.

Baptism followed their conversion, as we see throughout the New Testament. As Lydia and her household were baptized on their profession of faith in Jesus (16:15), so the jailer and his family were baptized following their declaration of faith (16:33). This was the pattern of the New Testament church demonstrated throughout the Book of Acts. Baptism followed the model of Jesus (Matthew 3:13–16) and signaled the union of a believer with Jesus (Rom. 6:3–8).

The conversion of the jailer is the first example in the Book of Acts of a person who became a believer out of raw paganism without the influence of Judaism. Before this, the Gentiles who believed were God-fearers like Cornelius. They were drawn to Judaism and were at least influenced by it. Or they were proselytes like Lydia, who had converted to Judaism. Too,

What Would You Say?

In a conversation with the new employee at work, you casually mention that you meet with a group of your neighbors every Thursday night to study the Bible. He asks whether you have time to get a latte at the coffee shop across the street after work.

When you settle in at your table, he says, *I have a lot of questions about Jesus. Since you go to this Bible study group, maybe you can answer some of them. Tell me, how does a person come into a relationship with Jesus Christ?* What would you say?

---

the Samaritans in Acts 8, although rejected by the Israelites, were part Israelite and were strongly influenced by the Jewish tradition. In contrast, the jailer was a pagan Roman with no apparent knowledge of or influence from the traditions of Judaism. Yet, like Lydia and the slave girl, he too was included in the *whosoever* of the invitation of the gospel.

Implications and Actions

At a Baptist meeting, I heard a pastor describe a visiting evangelist who had come to his church. On the first night of the services, the visiting evangelist singled out different groups in the church—anyone who gossiped, anyone who smoked, anyone who drank, etc. The visiting evangelist then told each group to get out because they were going to hell. Finally, the pastor moved to the pulpit, eased the visiting evangelist aside, and announced to his people: "All of you out there, come on back in, for it was just for such as you that Jesus died."

> Baptism followed their conversion as we see throughout the New Testament.

We need to advance that good news to those who are around us. We need to let everyone know that it was just for such as them that Jesus died. Or to paraphrase the statement made by my church member that I cited at the beginning of the lesson, we need to announce to the world that everyone is *God's kind of people*!

QUESTIONS

1. How would you have responded to the man in my church who described the people in our neighborhood as "not our kind of people"?

2. How selective do you think our churches are today in the people with whom we share the gospel?

3. What specific steps can your church take to relate the gospel to those who do not look like and dress like the members of your congregation?

4. What can you do as an individual to come in contact with people who really need to hear the gospel?

5. How do you respond when you hear that certain churches are targeting the kind of people they are trying to reach?

aug. 5-07

Focal Text
Acts 17:10–11, 16–34

Background
Acts 17:10–34

Main Idea
Churches need to extend the gospel to people who don't believe the Bible as well as to those who do.

Question to Explore
How can churches share the gospel with people who do not believe the Bible or have a high opinion of the church as previous generations did?

Study Aim
To identify implications for our church's ministry from how Paul shared the gospel with people who were skeptics and didn't believe the Bible

Study and Action Emphases
- Affirm the Bible as our authoritative guide for life and ministry
- Share the gospel with all people
- Develop a growing, vibrant faith
- Value all people as created in the image of God

LESSON TWELVE

Sharing the Gospel with Skeptics

Quick Read
When Paul presented the gospel in Athens, he changed his approach so he could connect more effectively with the distinctive audience in this pagan city.

A nice-looking couple met me at the church door at the end of the worship service. They introduced themselves and asked whether they could come by and talk with me. When they first sat down in my office, our conversation covered subjects of general interest. Gradually the conversation moved toward a discussion about the church.

I could tell that the young woman had little knowledge of what I was saying. So I focused my conversation more on her and eventually began to talk to her about Jesus. I told her that Jesus lived among us to reveal God to us. More personally, Jesus came to die for our sins.

At that point, the young lady stunned me with the question: "Is all of this written down somewhere?" I informed her that this story was indeed written down in the Bible. I opened my Bible to the table of contents and pointed to the Gospels, explaining that the story of Jesus was told in four different stories called Matthew, Mark, Luke, and John. I apologized, saying that I didn't mean to be too elementary for her. She responded, "I need you to be elementary. I don't have any idea what you are talking about."

This young woman reflects the biblical ignorance in American society today. Side by side with those who do not know anything about the Bible are those with the postmodern mindset who have rejected the authority of the Bible altogether. They know at least something of what the Bible says, but they just don't believe it, and neither do they accept it as authoritative for their lives.

When Paul arrived at Athens, the intellectual center of Greek and Roman culture, he faced the same skepticism. Geographically the city centered around a rocky mountain called the Acropolis. Culturally the city centered around an intellectual curiosity and an interest in science and philosophy. The challenge facing Paul in Athens, as well as in the other Greek/Roman cities, was to present the message of a Jewish rabbi who fulfilled God's promises to Israel in such a way that the message's universal relevance could be understood. Consequently, Paul took every opportunity available to share the gospel.

Acts 17:10–11, 16–34

[10]As soon as it was night, the brothers sent Paul and Silas away to Berea. On arriving there, they went to the Jewish synagogue. [11]Now the Bereans were of more noble character than the Thessalonians, for they received the message with great eagerness and examined the Scriptures every day to see if what Paul said was true.

. . . .

¹⁶While Paul was waiting for them in Athens, he was greatly distressed to see that the city was full of idols. ¹⁷So he reasoned in the synagogue with the Jews and the God-fearing Greeks, as well as in the marketplace day by day with those who happened to be there. ¹⁸A group of Epicurean and Stoic philosophers began to dispute with him. Some of them asked, "What is this babbler trying to say?" Others remarked, "He seems to be advocating foreign gods." They said this because Paul was preaching the good news about Jesus and the resurrection. ¹⁹Then they took him and brought him to a meeting of the Areopagus, where they said to him, "May we know what this new teaching is that you are presenting? ²⁰You are bringing some strange ideas to our ears, and we want to know what they mean." ²¹(All the Athenians and the foreigners who lived there spent their time doing nothing but talking about and listening to the latest ideas.)

²²Paul then stood up in the meeting of the Areopagus and said: "Men of Athens! I see that in every way you are very religious. ²³For as I walked around and looked carefully at your objects of worship, I even found an altar with this inscription: TO AN UNKNOWN GOD. Now what you worship as something unknown I am going to proclaim to you.

²⁴"The God who made the world and everything in it is the Lord of heaven and earth and does not live in temples built by hands. ²⁵And he is not served by human hands, as if he needed anything, because he himself gives all men life and breath and everything else. ²⁶From one man he made every nation of men, that they should inhabit the whole earth; and he determined the times set for them and the exact places where they should live. ²⁷God did this so that men would seek him and perhaps reach out for him and find him, though he is not far from each one of us. ²⁸'For in him we live and move and have our being.' As some of your own poets have said, 'We are his offspring.'

²⁹"Therefore since we are God's offspring, we should not think that the divine being is like gold or silver or stone—an image made by man's design and skill. ³⁰In the past God overlooked such ignorance, but now he commands all people everywhere to repent. ³¹For he has set a day when he will judge the world with justice by the man he has appointed. He has given proof of this to all men by raising him from the dead."

³²When they heard about the resurrection of the dead, some of them sneered, but others said, "We want to hear you again on this subject." ³³At that, Paul left the Council. ³⁴A few men became followers of Paul and believed. Among them was Dionysius, a member of the Areopagus, also a woman named Damaris, and a number of others.

Sharing in the Synagogue (17:10–11)

Before going to Athens, Paul stopped in the city of Berea. Berea was a part of the province of Macedonia, as was Philippi and Thessalonica. Again, Paul started in the synagogue, where he would likely find interest in his message about Jesus. The worshipers in the Berean synagogue were indeed interested in Paul's message.

Luke tells us that the Bereans "were of more noble character than the Thessalonians" (Acts 17:11). Paul's previous stop had been Thessalonica, the chief port and the capital city of the province. Paul's preaching there had met with some positive response initially. But instead of evaluating further Paul's message, the majority of the Jewish worshipers at Thessalonica had rejected it. They subsequently caused a riot that resulted in Paul's rapid exit from the city (17:10). But in Berea, Luke tells us, the people were "of more noble character" (17:11). Then he explains why he calls them noble. They were open-minded to the message of the gospel presented by Paul.

> To fulfill the challenge of Acts 1:8, we need to develop a strategy that intentionally will push us out of the church into the marketplace with the gospel.

Notice the two phrases Luke uses to describe the response of the Bereans. He says they "received the message" and then they "examined the Scriptures" (17:11). The "message" is the gospel concerning Jesus Christ. The essence of that message appears in most of the sermons preserved in the Book of Acts. This message builds around four basic elements, commonly referred to by New Testament scholars as the *kerygma*: the announcement that the time prophesied in the Old Testament had arrived; a description of the life, death, and resurrection of Jesus; identification of the Old Testament Scriptures whose promises Jesus fulfilled; and then a call to repentance. The message Paul presented to the synagogue worshipers in Berea no doubt included these same four ideas.

The "Scriptures" the Bereans examined are from what we know as the Old Testament. The New Testament writers over and over again declared that things happened in the life of Jesus "according to the Scriptures" or "in order that the Scriptures should be fulfilled." A good example is 1 Corinthians 15:3–4. Some passages of Scripture were evidently recognized as providing especially pointed testimony about Jesus. Among these Scriptures would have been the passages that spoke of the Suffering Servant, in Isaiah 42:1–4; 49:1–6; 50:4–9; and 52—53. The particular

references the Bereans examined are not identified. Whatever the particular references, though, the Berean Christians examined these Scriptures
to see whether Paul's proclamations about Jesus were valid.

Sharing in the Marketplace (17:16–18)

Soon those who had agitated the crowds in Thessalonica arrived in Berea
to stir up the crowds there as well. Silas and Timothy remained in Berea to
provide more instruction for the new believ-
ers, but Paul went to Athens (17:14).

The text implies that Paul did not intend
at that point to begin a mission to Athens.
He planned to wait until Silas and Timothy
joined him. However, he was so disturbed
by the idols all around the city that he could
not remain silent (17:16). He found the synagogue and shared the gospel with the Jewish
worshipers. Too, he also shared the gospel in "the marketplace day by day
with those who happened to be there" (17:17).

*We need to recognize
. . . that people in the
marketplace will often
be confused by our
message unless we take
great care to explain it.*

The marketplace was a square in the heart of the city where people
gathered to do business and to converse with their friends. The marketplace was the civic and social center of the city.

Idols and God

The Bible says that God made us in his own image, but the followers of the
religion of Greece created gods out of their own image. They made tangible the
pantheon of gods that resulted by creating many statues representing them.

What was true throughout the Greek empire during its glory days (fourth
century B.C.) was still true of Athens during the first century. An idol was an
image of a god used as an object of worship, and Athens was full of them. In
Paul's day more idols existed in the city of Athens than in the rest of Greece
put together. Too, in case the Athenians had missed one of the gods, they even
added an idol "TO AN UNKNOWN GOD" (Acts 17:23).

This display of idols provoked Paul into action. He countered these gods
crafted by human hands with the message of a Creator God who crafted
humanity and redeemed us through Jesus Christ.

Luke used the word "reasoned" to describe Paul's approach to sharing in both the synagogue and the marketplace. "Reasoned" translates a Greek word from which we get our word *dialogue*. This word pictures more a discussion than a formal presentation, more a dialogue than a declaration. As far as we can tell, this was a distinctly new strategy for Paul. In other places where he was forced out of the synagogue, Paul pursued other avenues for sharing the gospel, but in this case his strategy seemed to be intentional.

> From Paul, we learn that our methods for sharing the gospel might have to be changed. . . .

In the marketplace, Paul encountered a different kind of people from those who immediately connected with his message because of their Jewish heritage. Too, he encountered a different response from that of those in Berea who had eagerly listened to his message.

Among others, Paul's audience included "a group of Epicurean and Stoic philosophers" (17:18). Epicureanism was a way of thinking that centered in pleasure. It called for a life of tranquility and ease in this life because when death comes, the person no longer exists. Stoicism was a way of thinking that centered in harmony with nature. It called for a life of rational self-sufficiency that rose above circumstances and ignored the concerns of others.

These local philosophers were not impressed by either Paul's credentials or his message. They labeled Paul with two condescending terms (17:18). First, they accused him of being a "babbler." That translation may not be the best, for the word literally means *seed picker* and describes sparrows who survived by picking up seeds in the marketplace. The bird did not discriminate in its diet. It just picked up whatever pieces of grain it could find. So these critics accused Paul of being an intellectual sparrow, picking up bits and pieces of knowledge in an indiscriminate way and then spouting it out to his audience to impress others with his vast knowledge.

> . . . We must look for points of connection with those with whom we share the gospel. . . .

Second, they accused him of "advocating foreign gods." What foreign gods did Paul advocate? Clearly in his proclamation of Jesus as the Son of God, Paul would be presenting Jesus as a god. Apparently, the listeners mistakenly thought that "resurrection" was a goddess as well. So Paul's sharing in the marketplace seemed to raise as many questions as it provided answers.

What can we learn from Paul's experience in the marketplace? To begin with, Paul's intentionality provides a model for us to follow. To fulfill the challenge of Acts 1:8, we need to develop a strategy that intentionally will push us out of the church into the marketplace with the gospel.

We need to recognize, second, that people in the marketplace will often be confused by our message unless we take great care to explain it. Building relationships must be a key part of our strategy. Dialogue must be the method of our sharing.

Finally, Paul reminds us that we cannot be intimidated by the intellectual condescension from the pagans in the marketplace into changing our message to obtain their acceptance. We must continue to preach "the good news about Jesus and the resurrection" (17:18).

Sharing with the Philosophers (17:19–34)

Whether out of a curiosity to know more about these strange new teachings from Paul or out of concern that Paul's teachings would lead people astray, these philosophers called Paul before the Areopagus to explain his teaching. The Areopagus was both a place and a group of leaders. In our text, the word is used to refer to a group of leaders who were apparently the custodians of new ideas and the guardians against unwanted itinerant teachers. They invited Paul to share his ideas with them.

Paul's sermon before the Areopagus was brilliant in its rhetorical approach but decidedly different from Paul's other sermons recorded in the Book of Acts. In fact, its rhetorical brilliance is demonstrated in its distinct approach.

The message Paul delivered in Athens was different from the message he delivered at Antioch of Pisidia, for example (13:15–41). Granted, Luke probably gives us only a summary of these messages, but even from the summary the distinctiveness of the Athenian message is clear. At Athens, Paul quoted from Greek poets instead of quoting Hebrew prophets from the Old Testament. He emphasized God as Creator of the world instead of identifying God as the Redeemer of Israel. He began with an experience in the lives of the Athenians, not with a Scripture. Paul shaped his rhetorical

> *We must continue to proclaim that the crucified and risen Christ will provide eternal life to all who believe in him.*

How to Communicate the Gospel Today

How can we communicate the gospel effectively in a pagan world that is similar to the Athens of Paul's day? Consider these ideas and add others:

- Like the first-century Christians, the best approach is not to denounce other faiths but to proclaim Christ with all the power and persuasiveness at our disposal.
- Direct their attention to Jesus, giving them an opportunity to explore the richness of the Gospel accounts to get a clear picture of who Jesus is.
- Focus on our personal testimony and the change Christ has brought in our lives.

strategy to fit the different audiences. Paul's sermon at Athens was different from his previous preaching because his audience was different.

Paul ended the sermon by pointing the Athenians to Jesus and rooting his message in the resurrection. But he traveled a different pathway to arrive at that destination.

The response was different as well. Instead of many responding in faith and a few responding more cautiously, a few responded in faith while many made a more cautious—even a more caustic—response after Paul's sermon before the Areopagus (17:32–33).

I've heard preachers in the past who attributed the more cautious and caustic response of the Athenians to Paul's failure to "just preach Jesus." I think that misses the point. The different response can be attributed to the different audience. In Athens the soil had not been prepared through the instructions of the Old Testament law and the promises of the prophets.

Paul did not change the message as he shared the gospel in these more hostile settings. He did, though, change his methods because he realized that the message had to be presented in such a way that the audience could understand it and respond properly to it.

Implications and Actions

We can probably learn more from Paul's experience at Athens than from his experience in Antioch Pisidia (Acts 13), for we are living in a day when more and more people know less and less about the Bible. Both the skepticism of postmodernism and the tolerance of pluralism create a more challenging environment in which to talk about Jesus today.

The issue is not what we believe about Jesus. Our faith in the Jesus of the Gospels is firm. The issue is how we can communicate effectively the New Testament picture of Jesus to people who have little background in Christianity or who question Christianity's value and relevance.

. . . We are living in a day when more and more people know less and less about the Bible.

From Paul, we learn that our methods for sharing the gospel might have to be changed. We must look for points of connection with those with whom we share the gospel even as we avoid watering down the basic elements of our faith. We must continue to proclaim that the crucified and risen Christ will provide eternal life to all who believe in him.

QUESTIONS

1. What lessons can we learn from the Berean believers?

2. Why were Paul's critics so aggressive in trying to undermine his message of the gospel?

3. Compare Paul's sermon delivered at Pisidian Antioch (Acts 13:13–41) and the sermon he delivered at Athens (17:22–31). What are the differences? What are the similarities?

4. What can we do as believers to find points of contact for sharing Christ with people in our pluralistic, postmodern world, especially with people who do not have esteem for the Bible or who otherwise question the validity of the Christian faith?

Focal Text

Acts 19:8–10; 20:18–35

Background

Acts 19—20

Main Idea

Churches need to both minister effectively to Christians on the inside and reach out passionately to people on the outside.

Question to Explore

Which would you say your church needs to improve in most—ministering to Christians on the inside or reaching out to people on the outside?

Study Aim

To identify ways I need to help my church to both minister to Christians on the inside and reach out to people on the outside

Study and Action Emphases

- Affirm the Bible as our authoritative guide for life and ministry
- Share the gospel with all people
- Develop a growing, vibrant faith
- Value all people as created in the image of God
- Obey and serve Jesus by meeting physical, — spiritual, and emotional needs
- Equip people for servant leadership

LESSON THIRTEEN

Ministering Inside, Reaching Outside

Quick Read

The Apostle Paul provides a model of the Christian life, reflecting in his life what a Christian is to do and how churches should minister.

The Apostle Paul made an astounding statement to one of the churches to whom he wrote. He said: "Follow my example" (1 Corinthians 11:1). In this statement, Paul reflected on the power of models and articulated a truth that has been proven true in every arena of life throughout the ages. This significant life truth is that we learn best by observing. We are shaped most effectively not by what people tell us but by what they live before us. Paul understood that truth, and so he told the Corinthian Christians: *Do as I do.* "Follow my example."

Paul did not just tell these Christians, though, "Follow my example." Here is the entire quote from that passage: "Follow my example, as I follow the example of Christ." Paul was merely an expression of Christ, and Paul's example was worth following only as long as he reflected Christ.

Because Paul so closely followed Christ and so clearly reflected the spirit of Christ in his life, Paul remains a positive model for Christians today. What does it mean to be a Christian? How can we reflect Christ in our lives? What does the truly spiritual person look like? How can our churches minister best, most in line with Christ's Lordship? These questions provoke serious discussions today. Perhaps the best answer we can give to these questions is simply to say: "Follow the example of Paul, as he follows the example of Christ." In our text, Luke provides some snapshots of Paul as he modeled the Christian life.

Paul not only models the Christian life for us, though. Paul's ministry in these passages of Scripture also models for us a pattern for balanced church life—ministering inside while reaching outside.

Acts 19:8–10

[8]Paul entered the synagogue and spoke boldly there for three months, arguing persuasively about the kingdom of God. [9]But some of them became obstinate; they refused to believe and publicly maligned the Way. So Paul left them. He took the disciples with him and had discussions daily in the lecture hall of Tyrannus. [10]This went on for two years, so that all the Jews and Greeks who lived in the province of Asia heard the word of the Lord.

Acts 20:18–35

[18]When they arrived, he said to them: "You know how I lived the whole time I was with you, from the first day I came into the province

of Asia. [19]I served the Lord with great humility and with tears, although I was severely tested by the plots of the Jews. [20]You know that I have not hesitated to preach anything that would be helpful to you but have taught you publicly and from house to house. [21]I have declared to both Jews and Greeks that they must turn to God in repentance and have faith in our Lord Jesus.

[22]"And now, compelled by the Spirit, I am going to Jerusalem, not knowing what will happen to me there. [23]I only know that in every city the Holy Spirit warns me that prison and hardships are facing me. [24]However, I consider my life worth nothing to me, if only I may finish the race and complete the task the Lord Jesus has given me—the task of testifying to the gospel of God's grace.

[25]"Now I know that none of you among whom I have gone about preaching the kingdom will ever see me again. [26]Therefore, I declare to you today that I am innocent of the blood of all men. [27]For I have not hesitated to proclaim to you the whole will of God. [28]Keep watch over yourselves and all the flock of which the Holy Spirit has made you overseers. Be shepherds of the church of God, which he bought with his own blood. [29]I know that after I leave, savage wolves will come in among you and will not spare the flock. [30]Even from your own number men will arise and distort the truth in order to draw away disciples after them. [31]So be on your guard! Remember that for three years I never stopped warning each of you night and day with tears.

[32]"Now I commit you to God and to the word of his grace, which can build you up and give you an inheritance among all those who are sanctified. [33]I have not coveted anyone's silver or gold or clothing. [34]You yourselves know that these hands of mine have supplied my own needs and the needs of my companions. [35]In everything I did, I showed you that by this kind of hard work we must help the weak, remembering the words the Lord Jesus himself said: 'It is more blessed to give than to receive.'"

Paul's Teaching (19:8–10)

When Paul arrived in Ephesus, he began his ministry in the synagogue to fulfill a promise he had made on his earlier visit (Acts 18:19–21). At that time, Paul had received a receptive hearing in the synagogue, and those who attended requested an extended time of sharing. However, because Paul did not plan a long stay in Ephesus at that time, he promised he would be back to continue his teaching. He fulfilled that promise with this second visit. For three months he taught in the synagogue without any disturbance (19:8). This was his longest teaching time in the synagogue in any of the cities he evangelized.

But soon the honeymoon was over in Ephesus, and the detractors created a stir with their criticism of Paul and his message. However, this criticism did not silence Paul. He simply moved to a different venue. In a local lecture hall owned by a man named Tyrannus (19:9), he continued to teach about the kingdom of God. Here Paul taught for two years, and the influence of that teaching radiated throughout the province of Asia as word about Paul's teaching spread.

Notice that at this time the Christian faith was referred to as "the Way" and those who followed "the Way" were called "disciples" (19:9). Actually, when Paul was still the antagonist of the church and was passionately seeking to destroy the church rather than to develop it, Paul sought to imprison all who "belonged to the Way" (9:2). So this is not a new term to identify Christians. Even so, however, the term does not appear at all between that early reference in Acts 9:2 and the reference in our text. The term is appropriate because it pictures the Christian life as a journey with Jesus, an idea that echoes Jesus' initial invitation to the disciples to "follow me" (Matthew 4:19). The New Testament uses the word *disciples* in an official sense to identify the twelve individuals initially chosen to follow Jesus (Matt 10:1). But the term also was used in a general sense to refer to all followers of Jesus (Acts 6:1). This term is obviously used in that general sense in our text.

> We are shaped most effectively not by what people tell us but by what they live before us.

What can we learn from this picture of the Apostle Paul? We note his passion for sharing the message of Jesus with those who have never heard it to bring them into faith. We note, too, his commitment to sharing the message of Jesus with believers to develop them in their faith. We must continue to follow that pattern today.

Paul's Service (20:18–21)

The opposition increased until finally Paul decided to leave Ephesus "to go to Jerusalem, passing through Macedonia and Achaia" (Acts 19:21). However, he was not yet done sharing with the new Christians at Ephesus.

After several more months of ministry in the provinces of Macedonia and Asia, Paul and company sailed to Miletus (see 19:22—20:17). There he rendezvoused with the leaders from Ephesus, whom he had invited to meet him there. The focus of his message was not on accepting the gospel. These Ephesian Christians had already done that. Instead, Paul focused on how they should live out the gospel in their lives.

Paul's ministry . . . models for us a pattern for balanced church life—ministering inside while reaching outside.

Paul pointed to his own service, not to exalt himself but to encourage them. In a succinct summary, Paul identified the primary characteristics of his service for the Lord.

Transparency marked Paul's ministry among the Ephesians (20:18). He had no hidden agendas. He did not manipulate with misleading words. He did not play a part. Instead, his life was an open book.

Humility also characterized his ministry among them (20:19). Paul probably used this word in the distinctly Christian meaning of a recognition of our total inadequacy before and dependency on God. Nothing he did could be explained by his own power. His adequacy came from God.

Courage was another mark of Paul's ministry (20:19). Opposition did not deter him, and neither did critics discourage him. His fear of the Lord overcame all other fears.

The Kingdom of God

Paul spoke to the Ephesian believers "about the kingdom of God" (Acts 19:8). Even though the Book of Acts begins (1:3) and ends (28:31) by referring to the kingdom of God, that phrase does not appear often in between (see 8:12; 14:22).

Only at Ephesus does Luke tell us that the kingdom of God was the subject of Paul's preaching. On other occasions, Luke tells us that Paul was "preaching the gospel" (16:10; see 20:24). Luke uses both terms to describe the preaching of Philip (8:12; 8:40), indicating that these two terms were interchangeable.

For Luke, the gospel was the good news that in Jesus Christ God had established his kingdom on the earth and through the returning Christ would someday consummate his kingdom. Jesus had instructed the first disciples about the kingdom of God (1:3), and they had no doubt passed along his teaching. Paul continued that focus on the kingdom of God in his ministry among the Ephesian believers.

Most important, through all of his experiences, Paul remained *faithful* in his proclamation of the gospel (20:20–21). Whether engaged in conversations with individuals in their homes or preaching publicly, whether relating the gospel to Jews or to Gentiles, Paul never swayed from the central message of Jesus as the Savior of the world.

What can we learn from this picture of the Apostle Paul? We learn the importance of practicing what we preach. Living an authentically Christian life will give credibility to our message. Words without deeds will not attract anyone to the gospel. We must live out our faith with transparency, humility, and courage.

Paul's Future (20:22–27)

As Paul shared with the Ephesian Christians, he not only recalled his service among them. He also called their attention to what lay ahead. The future was clearly stormy, an insight Paul discerned from the Holy Spirit.

How can we reflect Christ in our lives?

Exactly how the Holy Spirit warned Paul about the hardships ahead is not known. Later, when Paul was in Caesarea, a prophet named Agabus came from Judea and predicted that Paul would be handed over to the Gentiles (21:10–11). The warning from Agabus didn't come until after Paul's conversation with the Ephesians in our text, however. So the method by which the Holy Spirit revealed to Paul what lay ahead remains a mystery.

More important than how Paul discerned what lay ahead is Paul's response. The key word is "however" (20:24). That word carries the same weight as *nevertheless*. Paul knew that danger lay ahead. Paul sensed that prison or even death might be in his near future. He would go to Jerusalem anyway, because being in the center of God's will was more important to Paul than personal safety. That is the impact of the word "however." Paul's top priority in life was to "finish the race" and to "complete the task" that Jesus had given him. That task was to proclaim the gospel of Jesus Christ to everyone who would hear. What Paul had done faithfully (20:27), he would continue to do, regardless of what happened to him personally.

What does the truly spiritual person look like?

How Would You Have Responded?

A young lady who indicated an interest in joining our church called for an appointment. When she sat down in my office, she said, *I'm considering joining this church, but I wanted to ask you a question first: Are you going to try to save me every week?* What do you think she meant by that question? How would you have responded?

What can we learn from this picture of the Apostle Paul? We see the importance of purpose. Paul simplified his life to a singular focus on his purpose. Consequently, he did not worry about personal safety. He was not concerned about comfort. Too, he did not waste his energy trying to control the circumstances of his life. All of those things were in God's hands. The only thing Paul could control was his unswerving commitment to the purpose for which he had been called. As it was for Paul, singleness of purpose should be the motivating passion of our lives.

Paul's Challenge (20:28–31)

From concern about his own future Paul moved to express concern for the future of the church at Ephesus. He urged the leaders of the Ephesian church to remain on the alert (20:28). Dangers abounded both outside and inside the church. So Paul reminded the leaders, whom he called both "overseers" and "shepherds" (20:28), of their responsibility to protect the body of believers from these

> *Living an authentically Christian life will give credibility to our message.*

dangers. Their responsibility was heightened by two things (20:28). First, the Holy Spirit had appointed them to their task, endowing them with the gift of leadership. Second, the church they were called to protect was valuable to God, for he had purchased it "with his own blood."

Paul provided a pattern for these leaders in his own example. He did not simply present the gospel to the Ephesians, establish a church, and then go on to other locales. Instead, he planted his life in Ephesus for three years, laying a theological and organizational structure that would prepare them for the challenges ahead (20:31).

Over the years as a pastor, I have found Paul's warning to be on target. Eternal vigilance is required to guard the church against threats that arise from both within and without.

When I was a young pastor, we started some home discipleship groups among the young adults in our church. These individuals were passionate about their faith and deeply committed to the church. I felt the discipleship groups would strengthen the church. Instead, they almost split the church. Because of inadequate supervision of these groups, some of the leaders introduced doctrines that confused the other members of the group and raised serious conflict in the church. I had failed to heed Paul's warning to "keep watch" (20:28) and "be on your guard" (20:31).

What can we learn from this picture of the Apostle Paul? Paul teaches us the need for diligence as leaders of the people of God. Because of the foibles of human nature and the persistent work of the Evil One, we must ever be on guard.

Paul's Commitment (20:32–35)

Paul concluded his address to his friends in the Ephesian church by committing them to the Lord with the full assurance that God would provide adequately for their needs through his grace. Repeatedly, Paul assured those whom he led to the Lord that God's grace was sufficient to provide for all their needs. His Letter to the Ephesians is filled with such assurances (see Ephesians 1:7–8; 2:5–8; 4:7). Perhaps the classic statement of this promise was his word to the Philippians: "And my God will meet all your needs according to his glorious riches in Christ Jesus" (Philippians 4:19). God's grace would be sufficient to build up the Ephesian leaders in the faith and protect their eternal inheritance, as it had been sufficient for Paul (see 2 Corinthians 12:9).

Words without deeds will not attract anyone to the gospel.

Yet, this assurance of God's sufficient grace did not release these Ephesian leaders from their responsibility to give themselves to God and to the work to which God had called them. As leaders, their primary concern was to be neither the blessings God could give to them nor even the respect the church members could give to them. Rather their primary concern was to be what they could give to the church. Paul established this call to selfless giving first of all in his own example (20:33–35). Then he established this call to selfless giving in one of Jesus' sayings that is not recorded in the Gospels: "It is more blessed to give than to receive" (20:35).

What can we learn from this picture of the Apostle Paul? Paul teaches us that leadership is not first of all a privilege but a responsibility. Leadership is not about what we can get but about what we can give. In the world, leaders often are concerned with their own glory, but Jesus said this should not be the case among those who are leaders in the kingdom of God. Instead, in his kingdom, Jesus explained, "Whoever wants to become great among you must be your servant" (Mark 10:43).

QUESTIONS

1. Who are some of the people who have influenced you by the model of their Christian life?

2. Do you think the church today places too much emphasis on sharing the gospel with those who have never heard it or too much emphasis on addressing those who have already heard it?

3. Why is it important for us to live out our faith?

4. What is the primary purpose of the Christian life?

5. Can you recall a time when you let down your guard and suffered the consequences?

6. In what ways should leaders in the church be different from leaders outside the church?

Focal Text
Luke 24:13–35

Background
Luke 24

Main Idea
As we experience the resurrected Jesus, we are able to make him known to others.

Question to Explore
How can we more readily experience and more willingly share the good news about Jesus?

Study Aim
To find ways to experience and share the good news of the resurrected Jesus

Study and Action Emphases
- Affirm the Bible as our authoritative guide for life and ministry
- Share the gospel with all people
- Develop a growing, vibrant faith

EASTER LESSON

"The Lord Has Risen Indeed!"

Quick Read
Search for the risen Jesus, always hidden in plain sight, so you will be able to share him with others.

Life is filled with challenges. Expressing faith in Jesus Christ as your Lord and Savior is a challenge. All around you are experiences and people who discourage you from living by faith. Within you, doubts surface and questions arise.

This Easter may find you involved in a journey down a road called "familiar" with a friend, discussing the common occurrences of your lives. You may be facing challenges, trying to encourage each other in the midst of your sadness. You may find reasons to talk about Jesus and think about Jesus without truly understanding how the news of his resurrection transforms your experience of life. Yet, because of Jesus' resurrection, every challenge in your life is less challenging. This is the situation described by Luke, as two of Jesus' followers walked from Jerusalem to Emmaus—about a seven-mile journey.

Luke is a wonderful storyteller. This story of the Emmaus walk is one of the most complete and well-written stories in Scripture. It does not appear in any of the other Gospels.[1]

These disciples give us a transcript for our human experience. They were facing a challenge of faith. Once they accepted the reality of Jesus' resurrection, they must share their experience with others. Welcome to the good news!

Luke 24:13–35

[13] Now that same day two of them were going to a village called Emmaus, about seven miles from Jerusalem. [14] They were talking with each other about everything that had happened. [15] As they talked and discussed these things with each other, Jesus himself came up and walked along with them; [16] but they were kept from recognizing him.

[17] He asked them, "What are you discussing together as you walk along?"

They stood still, their faces downcast. [18] One of them, named Cleopas, asked him, "Are you only a visitor to Jerusalem and do not know the things that have happened there in these days?"

[19] "What things?" he asked.

"About Jesus of Nazareth," they replied. "He was a prophet, powerful in word and deed before God and all the people. [20] The chief priests and our rulers handed him over to be sentenced to death, and they crucified him; [21] but we had hoped that he was the one who was going to redeem Israel. And what is more, it is the third day since all this took place. [22] In addition, some of our women amazed us. They went to the tomb early this morning [23] but didn't find his body. They came and told us that they had seen a vision of angels, who said he was alive. [24] Then some of our companions went to the tomb and found it just as the women had said, but him they did not see."

[25] He said to them, "How foolish you are, and how slow of heart to believe all that the prophets have spoken! [26] Did not the Christ have to suffer these things and then enter his glory?" [27] And beginning with Moses and all the Prophets, he explained to them what was said in all the Scriptures concerning himself.

[28] As they approached the village to which they were going, Jesus acted as if he were going farther. [29] But they urged him strongly, "Stay with us, for it is nearly evening; the day is almost over." So he went in to stay with them.

[30] When he was at the table with them, he took bread, gave thanks, broke it and began to give it to them. [31] Then their eyes were opened and they recognized him, and he disappeared from their sight. [32] They asked each other, "Were not our hearts burning within us while he talked with us on the road and opened the Scriptures to us?"

[33] They got up and returned at once to Jerusalem. There they found the Eleven and those with them, assembled together [34] and saying, "It is true! The Lord has risen and has appeared to Simon." [35] Then the two told what had happened on the way, and how Jesus was recognized by them when he broke the bread.

Hidden in Plain Sight (24:13–16)

In the dining hall at a church-related college was a large bowl of apples with this sign: "Take only one—God is watching!" At the other end of the dining hall was a large container of broken cookies. Some quick-thinking student had installed a sign that read: "Take all you want. God is watching the apples."

Where is God? What is getting God's attention today? Every generation, every person, embarks on a journey to identify the active presence of God in the midst of life's steps, successes, and sorrows.

Several years ago, I sat on a bench in a shopping mall while my wife completed some errands. Nearby was a playground where children were playing in groups. Between the playground and my position on the bench was an elderly woman in a wheelchair. Her eyes were fixed on the children as two little girls started singing a song. The elderly woman smiled and swayed her body to their tempo. The children were oblivious to their audience. They never noticed the woman appreciating their song. My position, in that moment in time, allowed me to watch her watching the children.

This is our position as we read Luke 24:13–35. We are able to observe the Emmaus walkers from a distance. We already know of Jesus' resurrection. We are watching them and watching Jesus watch them, knowing they were oblivious to who their traveling companion was. Yet, Jesus was there, hidden in plain sight in their world.

> . . . Because of Jesus' resurrection, every challenge in your life is less challenging.

What kept these disciples from recognizing Jesus Christ? They were witnessing the resurrected Jesus and did not know him. Were they unable to recognize Jesus because of their grief, their disappointment, their fear, their focus on each other, or their concentration on their pre-determined destination and their desire to reach home? Jesus inquired about the cause of their sadness. It's just like Jesus to touch the heart of the matter that is setting the pace of our walk.

As you read this story, notice the three speeds of the walk of these two disciples. Like a shifting transmission, there is the slow speed as they walk along and are sad over the death of Jesus; there is the middle gear, as Jesus joins their journey; and there is the fast speed as they hurry back to Jerusalem to witness of Jesus' resurrection and appearance to them.

It was the afternoon of the Sunday when Jesus was raised from the dead. These two disciples of Jesus were walking along burdened by the realities of life. Meanwhile, Jesus was hidden in plain sight all along. Welcome to the experience of Easter!

The Rest of the Story (24:17–24)

Does it seem odd to you that these two disciples were trying to tell Jesus what had happened when they didn't have a clue? This is not uncommon. Often in today's church, explanations of Scripture and of current events are offered, without including the perspective of God as revealed through Jesus Christ. Unless we are careful, we can assume we have all the answers when we are not even asking the right questions.

For decades, many Americans have listened to radio commentator Paul Harvey tell stories. He raises your interest with the first part of the story.

Then he goes to a commercial, followed by "the rest of the story." Cleopas and his companion presented to Jesus their understanding of the events of the past three days. Then Jesus offered them the rest of the story.

I heard a story while in Kenya recently of a man who stepped into a shop of the open market. He was looking for a handmade cross. The man in charge of the shop asked the shopper, "Do you want a blank cross, or do you want one with a little man on it?"

While Cleopas and the other disciple didn't understand the meaning of Jesus'

What is getting God's attention today?

death on the cross, they knew the reality of it. They knew of Jesus' crucifixion, and they were still more focused on the cross than on the stories of Jesus' empty grave. Yet, here we are on Easter morning, celebrating Jesus' resurrection. On this day, we are more focused on the empty grave than on the cross.

Expressing your appreciation and thankfulness for the cross of Jesus Christ is important. Jesus willingly went to the cross and died your death. But you must move beyond the cross and focus your life on the empty grave of Jesus and on the resurrected Jesus. After all, you are intended to be one of God's Easter people!

If you focus more on the cross than on the resurrected Jesus, you will forever be on your way to Emmaus without a stirring in your heart. The resurrection of Jesus gives the cross its victory.

I once saw a sign that read, "Think small; we can deal with that." When you live as one of God's Easter people, you will not be satisfied with small thoughts. Because of Jesus' resurrection, you know the worst thing to happen is never the last thing that happens. You know the worst thing that could ever happen to you has already happened, and his grave just outside Jerusalem is empty. You know the rest of the story.

"Have Faith in God"

In the 1930s, when the depression was at its most devastating point, the gospel songwriter B.B. McKinney (who grew up in Winn Parish, Louisiana, and then ministered in various ways in Texas before serving at the Baptist Sunday School Board in Nashville) wrote these words that have encouraged many people, "Have faith in God when your pathway is lonely. . . ."[3] The two discouraged travelers on the way to Emmaus needed to hear that message. Do you?

Jesus Speaks to the Slow of Heart (24:25–27)

In recent years, people have popularized the question, *What would Jesus do?* While this is a good question, there are some better questions: *What is Jesus doing inside of me, and what is Jesus calling me to be and do in the world? How can I be obedient to Christ's Lordship in my life as Christ shapes me and seeks to shape the world through me?*

Jesus started by asking these disciples a question (24:17): "What are you discussing together as you walk along?" Then, in verse 25, we read about Jesus saying to them, "How foolish you are, and how slow of heart to believe all that the prophets have spoken!"

Some of the good news of Easter is that Jesus speaks to the "slow of heart." That is us! We are these disciples on the road to our familiar past. We tend to focus on the crucifixion more than the resurrection. We tend to be overcome by the worst of moments and fail to look for the ways God is working to bring hope and life from grief, suffering, shame, pain, death, and chaos. We tend to focus on darkness in the midst of the dawn. We are the "slow of heart."

> The resurrection of Jesus gives the cross its victory.

These two disciples, walking to Emmaus, thought the death of Jesus on the cross represented failure. Jesus rebuked their slowness of heart. Then he explained to them everything about himself. Jesus not only explained Scripture to them, but also he spoke of himself as the fulfillment of Scripture.

Journey Beyond Your Destination (24:28–35)

Archaeologists have not yet determined the exact location of Emmaus. But you know the location of Emmaus, don't you? Emmaus is the place you go to have a "pity party" when things go wrong. Emmaus is your temporary hiding place, when you do not grasp your identity as one of God's Easter people. Emmaus is where you go when you allow cynicism and defeat to take over your life.

When you are tempted to journey to the destination of Emmaus, think twice. Invite Jesus into your life, and give your life to him. When you are wronged, defeated, or abused, you can either allow your thoughts and feelings to overshadow the Spirit of Christ within you or you can

Who Needs Your Help?

Make a list of those people who come to your mind in response to this question: *Who comes to mind when you think of people who need the risen Christ in you to offer them words and ministry of hope, encouragement, and comfort?*

---

allow the Spirit of Christ within you to overshadow your thoughts and feelings.

When you have an aching heart, when your spirit is low, you will find a companion comes alongside you. It is Jesus hidden in plain sight. Do you remember when you prayed to have a friend and someone showed up? That was Jesus hidden in plain sight. Do you remember when you were discouraged and a note or phone call arrived? That was Jesus hidden in plain sight. Do you remember when you questioned whether anyone really understood, and then a person looked through your eyes into your spirit and empathized with you? That was Jesus hidden in plain sight. God, in Christ, walks alongside you with wounded feet. God, in Christ, is always present but never intrusive.

These two disciples intended to go to Emmaus. However, they journeyed beyond their destination. When they reached their destination, they recognized Jesus. They sensed a warming in their spirits. Then they went beyond Emmaus, returning to Jerusalem to witness of their experience. They had been with the risen Jesus, who was hidden in plain sight.

> *Because of Jesus' resurrection, you know the worst thing to happen is never the last thing that happens.*

The experience of these disciples was never written down into a doctrinal statement. They did not see their experience to be theological dogma. For them, the experience of Christ was not a paper theology; it was a living relationship. That was what empowered them to journey beyond their destination. Experiencing the risen Christ does that to a person. It carries a person beyond his or her intentions to the intentions of God.

Each Advent and Christmas season, we love to hear a soloist sing the spiritual, "Sweet little Jesus boy, we didn't know who you was."[2] This same God who came incognito in a manger walks your Emmaus Road with you. Take courage, God's Easter people; Jesus Christ is hidden in plain sight in your life.

157

So, offer hope to your family and friends. Speak words of encouragement to the grieving. Embrace with words of comfort those who are broken by tragedy. Offer light to those who are ashamed. Remind the suffering that Christ is with them. Remember, Christ in you is the Christ hidden in plain sight.

> *They had been with the risen Jesus, who was hidden in plain sight.*

When you recognize Jesus in the difficult moments of life, he stirs you to set your sights on places beyond where you were going. As you experience the risen Christ who is always hidden in plain sight, you are able to share him with others along the familiar roads of life.

Yes, Christ is risen. He is risen indeed!

QUESTIONS

1. Why is it important that Luke included this incident in his Gospel? What unique insights does this account of Jesus' resurrection and its implications for our lives offer us?

2. Have you ever experienced Jesus hidden in plain sight? How?

3. Why do you think we often tend to focus more on grief, sadness, and fear than on hope, healing, and faith?

4. What can we do to see God in the midst of dark days?

5. Discuss each phrase. You are saved

    a. from sin and death

    b. to righteousness and eternal life

    c. for discipleship and missional living

6. How is your day-to-day life different because of Jesus' resurrection?

NOTES

1. Unless otherwise indicated, all Scripture quotations in this lesson are from the New International Version.
2. "Sweet Little Jesus Boy." Words and music by Robert MacGimsey.
3. "Have Faith in God." Words and music by B.B. McKinney.

Our Next New Study
(Available for use beginning June 2007)

JOB, ECCLESIASTES, HABAKKUK, LAMENTATIONS:
Dealing with Hard Times

Additional Resources for Studying the Book of Job[1]

W. H. Bellinger, Jr. *The Testimony of Poets and Sages: The Psalms and Wisdom Literature.* Macon, Georgia: Smyth and Helwys Publishing, Inc., 1997.

J. Gerald Janzen. *Job.* Interpretation: A Bible Commentary for Teaching and Preaching. Atlanta, Georgia: John Knox Press, 1985.

Carol A. Newsom. "Job." *The New Interpreter's Bible.* Volume IV. Nashville: Abingdon Press, 1996.

Ralph L. Smith. *Job: A Study in Providence and Faith.* Nashville, Tennessee: Convention Press, 1971.

John D. W. Watts, John Joseph Owens, Marvin E. Tate, Jr. "Job." *The Broadman Bible Commentary.* Volume 4. Nashville, Tennessee: Broadman Press, 1971.

Additional Resources for Studying the Book of Ecclesiastes

James L. Crenshaw. *Ecclesiastes.* The Old Testament Library. Philadelphia: The Westminster Press, 1987.

Wayne H. Peterson. "Ecclesiastes." *The Broadman Bible Commentary.* Volume 5. Nashville, Tennessee: Broadman Press, 1971.

W. Sibley Towner. "Ecclesiastes." *The New Interpreter's Bible.* Volume V. Nashville: Abingdon Press, 1997.

Additional Resources for Studying the Book of Habakkuk

Elizabeth Achtemeier. "Habakkuk." *Nahum—Malachi.* Interpretation: A Bible Commentary for Teaching and Preaching. Atlanta, Georgia: John Knox Press, 1986.

D. Waylon Bailey. "Habakkuk." *Micah, Nahum, Habakkuk, Zephaniah.* The New American Commentary. Nashville, Tennessee: Broadman and Holman Publishers, 1998.

D. David Garland. "Habakkuk." *The Broadman Bible Commentary.* Volume 7. Nashville, Tennessee: Broadman Press, 1972.

Theodore Hiebert. "Habakkuk." *The New Interpreter's Bible.* Volume VII. Nashville: Abingdon Press, 1996.

Additional Resources for Studying the Book of Lamentations

Robert B. Laurin. "Lamentations." *The Broadman Bible Commentary.* Volume 6. Nashville, Tennessee: Broadman Press, 1971.

Kathleen M. O'Connor. "The Book of Lamentations." *The New Interpreter's Bible.* Volume VI. Nashville: Abingdon Press, 2001.

NOTES

1. Listing a book does not imply full agreement by the writers or BAPTISTWAY PRESS® with all of its comments.

How to Order More Bible Study Materials

It's easy! Just fill in the following information. For additional Bible study materials, see www.baptistwaypress.org or get a complete order form of available materials by calling 1-866-249-1799 or e-mailing baptistway@bgct.org.

Title of item	Price	Quantity	Cost
This Issue:			
Acts: Toward Being a Missional Church—Study Guide (BWP001013)	$2.75	_____	_____
Acts: Toward Being a Missional Church—Large Print Study Guide (BWP001014)	$2.85	_____	_____
Acts: Toward Being a Missional Church—Teaching Guide (BWP001015)	$3.25	_____	_____
Additional Issues Available:			
Genesis 12—50: Family Matters—Study Guide (BWP000034)	$1.95	_____	_____
Genesis 12—50: Family Matters—Large Print Study Guide (BWP000032)	$1.95	_____	_____
Genesis 12—50: Family Matters—Teaching Guide (BWP000035)	$2.45	_____	_____
Leviticus, Numbers, Deuteronomy—Study Guide (BWP000053)	$2.35	_____	_____
Leviticus, Numbers, Deuteronomy—Large Print Study Guide (BWP000052)	$2.35	_____	_____
Leviticus, Numbers, Deuteronomy—Teaching Guide (BWP000054)	$2.95	_____	_____
Joshua, Judges—Study Guide (BWP000047)	$2.35	_____	_____
Joshua, Judges—Large Print Study Guide (BWP000046)	$2.35	_____	_____
Joshua, Judges—Teaching Guide (BWP000048)	$2.95	_____	_____
1 and 2 Samuel—Study Guide (BWP000002)	$2.35	_____	_____
1 and 2 Samuel—Large Print Study Guide (BWP000001)	$2.35	_____	_____
1 and 2 Samuel—Teaching Guide (BWP000003)	$2.95	_____	_____
Psalms and Proverbs: Songs and Sayings of Faith—Study Guide (BWP001000)	$2.75	_____	_____
Psalms and Proverbs: Songs and Sayings of Faith—Large Print Study Guide (BWP001001)	$2.85	_____	_____
Psalms and Proverbs: Songs and Sayings of Faith—Teaching Guide (BWP001002)	$3.25	_____	_____
Matthew: Jesus' Teachings—Study Guide (BWP000069)	$2.35	_____	_____
Matthew: Jesus' Teachings—Large Print Study Guide (BWP000068)	$2.35	_____	_____
Matthew: Jesus' Teachings—Teaching Guide (BWP000070)	$2.95	_____	_____
Jesus in the Gospel of Mark—Study Guide (BWP000066)	$1.95	_____	_____
Jesus in the Gospel of Mark—Large Print Study Guide (BWP000065)	$1.95	_____	_____
Jesus in the Gospel of Mark—Teaching Guide (BWP000067)	$2.45	_____	_____
Luke: Journeying to the Cross—Study Guide (BWP000057)	$2.35	_____	_____
Luke: Journeying to the Cross—Large Print Study Guide (BWP000056)	$2.35	_____	_____
Luke: Journeying to the Cross—Teaching Guide (BWP000058)	$2.95	_____	_____
The Gospel of John: The Word Became Flesh—Study Guide (BWP001008)	$2.75	_____	_____
The Gospel of John: The Word Became Flesh—Large Print Study Guide (BWP001009)	$2.85	_____	_____
The Gospel of John: The Word Became Flesh—Teaching Guide (BWP001010)	$3.25	_____	_____
1 Corinthians—Study Guide (BWP000004)	$1.95	_____	_____
1 Corinthians—Teaching Guide (BWP000006)	$2.45	_____	_____
2 Corinthians: Taking Ministry Personally—Study Guide (BWP000008)	$2.35	_____	_____
2 Corinthians: Taking Ministry Personally—Large Print Study Guide (BWP000007)	$2.35	_____	_____
2 Corinthians: Taking Ministry Personally—Teaching Guide (BWP000009)	$2.95	_____	_____

1, 2 Timothy, Titus, Philemon—*Study Guide* (BWP000092) $2.75   _____ _____
1, 2 Timothy, Titus, Philemon—*Large Print Study Guide*
  (BWP000091) $2.85   _____ _____
1, 2 Timothy, Titus, Philemon—*Teaching Guide* (BWP000093) $3.25   _____ _____
Hebrews and James—*Study Guide* (BWP000037) $1.95   _____ _____
Hebrews and James—*Teaching Guide* (BWP000038) $2.45   _____ _____
Revelation—*Study Guide* (BWP000084) $2.35   _____ _____
Revelation—*Large Print Study Guide* (BWP000083) $2.35   _____ _____
Revelation—*Teaching Guide* (BWP000085) $2.95   _____ _____

Coming for use beginning June 2007

Job, Ecclesiastes, Habakkuk, Lamentations: *Dealing with
  Hard Times*—*Study Guide* (BWP001016) $2.75   _____ _____
Job, Ecclesiastes, Habakkuk, Lamentations: *Dealing with
  Hard Times*—*Large Print Study Guide* (BWP001017) $2.85   _____ _____
Job, Ecclesiastes, Habakkuk, Lamentations: *Dealing with
  Hard Times*—*Teaching Guide* (BWP001018) $3.25   _____

Cost of items (Order value)   _____
Processing fee (1% of Cost of Items)   _____
Shipping charges (see chart*)   _____
TOTAL   _____

Standard (UPS/Mail) Shipping Charges*	
Order Value	Shipping charge
$.01—$9.99	$5.00
$10.00—$19.99	$6.00
$20.00—$39.99	$7.00
$40.00—$79.99	$8.00
$80.00—$99.99	$11.00
$100.00—$129.99	$13.00
$130.00—$149.99	$17.00
$150.00—$199.99	$20.00
$200.00—$299.99	$25.00
$300.00 and up	10% of order value

*Plus, applicable taxes for individuals and other taxable entities (not churches) within Texas will be added. Please call 1-866-249-1799 if the exact amount is needed prior to ordering.

Please allow three weeks for standard delivery. For express shipping service: Call 1-866-249-1799 for information on additional charges.

YOUR NAME

PHONE

YOUR CHURCH

DATE ORDERED

MAILING ADDRESS

CITY

STATE   ZIP CODE

MAIL this form with your check for the total amount to
BAPTISTWAY PRESS, Baptist General Convention of Texas,
333 North Washington, Dallas, TX 75246-1798
(Make checks to "Baptist Executive Board.")
OR, **FAX** your order anytime to: 214-828-5376, and we will bill you.
OR, **CALL** your order toll-free: 1-866-249-1799
(M-Th 8:30 a.m.-8:30 p.m.; Fri 8:30 a.m.-5:00 p.m.), and we will bill you.
OR, **E-MAIL** your order to our internet e-mail address:
baptistway@bgct.org, and we will bill you.
OR, **ORDER ONLINE** at www.baptistwaypress.org.
We look forward to receiving your order! Thank you!